In Pursuit of Doris Lessing

Nine Nations Reading

Edited by

CLAIRE SPRAGUE

*Visiting Professor of English, New York University,
and Professor Emeritus of Brooklyn College,
The City University of New York*

St. Martin's Press   New York

© The Macmillan Press Ltd 1990
Editorial matter and selection © Claire Sprague 1990

First published in the United States of America in 1990

Printed in Great Britain

ISBN 0–312–04713–4

Library of Congress Cataloging-in-Publication Data
In pursuit of Doris Lessing: nine nations reading /
    edited by Claire Sprague.
        p.   cm.
     ISBN 0–312–04713–4
     1. Lessing, Doris, 1919–   —Criticism and interpretation.
  I. Sprague, Claire.
  PR6023.E833Z7   1990
  823′.914—dc20
                                                        90–8106
                                                          CIP

IN PURSUIT OF DORIS LESSING

Contents

Contents

Acknowledgements

All of us who have written about Doris Lessing have learned from one another. My thanks to that exceptionally collaborative community.

For this volume I wish to thank all of the contributors and especially Lorna Peterson, Virginia Tiger, and Ellen Cronan Rose for their help in various phases of its preparation – finding the right title, reading my introduction, and talking through the usual minor and major aches that accompany the making of a book.

As always, my son Jesse participates in my work in ways both mysterious and self-evident. In the choice of the cover photograph, his eye was truer than mine.

My very special thanks to Dee Seligman who first used that perfect title, 'In Pursuit of Doris Lessing', in print and who has graciously permitted me to use it again for this volume.

Notes on the Contributors

Eve Bertelsen, a Senior Lecturer at the University of Cape Town, completed her doctorate at the University of London. She has edited *Doris Lessing*, no. 5 in the Southern Africa Literature Series (Johannesburg, 1985) and also written a book on Charles Dickens as well as articles on Lessing, D. H. Lawrence and other writers. In her appearances in the South African press and over South African television, she has talked about women, advertising and African literature.

Anthony Chennells was born in Zimbabwe and has lectured for many years in the Department of English at the University of Zimbabwe. He has made a comprehensive study of Southern Rhodesian settler novels and has published on these and other aspects of Southern African writing.

Fernando Galván Reula is Lecturer in English Literature at the University of La Laguna (Tenerife, Spain). His latest publications include an edition and translation of Graham Greene's *The Quiet American* (Madrid, 1987) and *Formas nuevas en la ficción británica contemporánea: David Lodge, Ian McEwan y Salman Rushdie* (La Laguna, 1988). The November 1988 issue of the *Revista Canaria de Estudios Ingleses*, of which he is the editor, is dedicated to recent British fiction.

Clare Hanson is Senior Lecturer in English at the College of St Paul and St Mary, Cheltenham. She has worked on the short story and on Katherine Mansfield. Her books include *Short Stories and Short Fictions, 1880–1980* and *The Critical Writings of Katherine Mansfield*. She has published on a variety of women writers and on feminist theory and is currently preparing a book on Virginia Woolf for the Macmillan Women Writers Series.

Nicole Ward Jouve is French and now lives in England. She has written fiction (*Shades of Grey*), criticism in English (*Colette* and *Baudelaire*), essays on Lessing, Simone de Beauvoir and Virginia Woolf, and a study of a mass murderer ('*The Streetcleaner'*: *The*

Yorkshire Ripper Case on Trial). She is Professor of English and Related Literatures and Women's Studies at York University.

Mona Knapp has a PhD in German literature and is the author of *Doris Lessing* (New York, 1984), and of monographs and articles on modern German and Commonwealth literature, as well as textbooks and reviews. She currently teaches German at a private school and is the associate editor of the *Doris Lessing Newsletter*.

Lorna M. Peterson is associate coordinator of Five Colleges, Incorporated (Amherst, Mass.) about which she has written a brief history, *Glancing Backward: Twenty Five Years of Cooperation* (1984). She has taught courses on contemporary women's fiction and women in Russian literature. She holds a PhD in Slavic Languages and Literature from Yale University.

Ellen Cronan Rose teaches English and Women's Studies at Drexel University. A former president of the Doris Lessing Society, she has published *The Tree Outside the Window: Doris Lessing's 'Children of Violence'* and articles on Lessing. With Carey Kaplan, she has edited *Doris Lessing: The Alchemy of Survival* and *Approaches to Teaching Lessing's 'The Golden Notebook'*.

Claire Sprague is a Professor Emeritus of Brooklyn College, CUNY, and a Visiting Professor at New York University. Her most recent book is *Rereading Doris Lessing: Narrative Strategies of Doubling and Repetition* (1987). She has served as president of the Doris Lessing Society (1980–2) and editor of the *Doris Lessing Newsletter* (1982–8). Her other published work includes *Critical Essays on Doris Lessing* (co-editor), *Virginia Woolf* (editor), and books and articles about various American writers. She is currently general editor of G. K. Hall's series on the impact of feminist theory on the arts and sciences.

Virginia Tiger is a Professor of English at Rutgers University (Newark) where she directs the Graduate English Program. She has written articles and reviews about contemporary British and American literature. Her books include *William Golding: The Dark Fields of Discovery* and *Everywoman*. She is also the co-editor of *Critical Essays on Doris Lessing* and a frequent contributor to the *Doris Lessing Newsletter*.

Introduction

Doris Lessing: 'In the World, But Not of It'

CLAIRE SPRAGUE

Doris Lessing has more than once used the Sufi saying 'in the world, but not of it'. The phrase bristles with ironies. For the reader who accepts Lessing's view of herself as once a realist and now a fabulist, it is likely to mean she has left this world for another one. But the phrase can also be taken to define Lessing's much earlier paradoxical behaviour as both participant and observer, both activist and bystander. Her earlier political engagements – at least since her departure from Zimbabwe (then Rhodesia) – were always carefully chosen. She wrote stories, letters, commentary, demonstrated, marched, but she stayed far away from day-to-day work in a political party. Today, as an open advocate of Sufi ideas and of the rebel Afghans, she continues to resist more formal submersion in her newer causes. Her partici-pation is none the less political and in the world by contrast with the 'not of it' half of the Sufi phase which suggests retreat from the world, the kind of detachment that mystical traditions have preached for millennia. Lessing insists on the double face of the Sufi saying, on its active as well as its detached half, placing herself outside the general human inability to believe 'in the combination of the mystic and the practical' ('In the World, Not of It', *SPV*, p. 133). Sufi is not, she clarifies for the uninitiate, 'contemptuous of the world' ('In the World', p. 133).

But the paradox of being in and out of the world at the same time is not confined to Sufi thought. It has appeared outside of mystical, prophetic, and religious thought. Poets have, for example, talked about the double face of artistic genesis. Wordsworth's 'emotion recollected in tranquillity' can be cited, or Frost's 'Fire and Ice'. Both suggest the simultaneous immersion and distance that characterise the artist's transformation of experience into art. We can see Lessing nod approvingly at this enlargement of

1

the paradoxical Sufi phrase. It suits her belief that Sufism 'is continuously in operation in every culture', although 'not necessarily' under its own name ('In the World', p. 129). Her stance, so typical of the true believer, has its special ironies, for Lessing's earlier Marxism was always sceptical, conditional, ironic.

If we place Lessing's essay 'The Small Personal Voice' (1957) against her durable global concerns, we construct another apparently irreconcilable but actually permanently interactive equation. The small personal voice in Lessing's essay is consumed with the problem of its relation to public facts and public voices. In that essay, Lessing laments, for example, the 'profoundly parochial' (*SPV*, p. 17) nature of English society and culture and calls for an international sensibility that imbeds the newest and surely the most painful and ironic source of our contemporary global kinship, 'the kinship of possible destruction' ('SPV', p. 9). Today's newspaper calls the atmosphere 'our global commons' and worries about MAD, or mutually assured destruction. Global destruction by nuclear or ecological disaster(s) will not discriminate; it will not favour one people, one nation, one race or one language over another. It makes us one people, albeit in a negative mode.

Long before the press spoke of 'our global commons' or anyone had coined the acronym MAD, Lessing thought of the world as her and our country ('SPV', p. 17). She has wanted to have and she has secured a global voice that seems the reverse of small and personal. From the beginning of her long career, she has attracted the common as well as the scholarly reader, men as well as woman, and third-world readers black and white. Given the gap between 'high' culture and 'middle' or 'low' culture, such a range of readers is astonishing. A few years ago *The Golden Notebook* sold its millionth copy. Translations of Lessing's fiction keep appearing all over the world. In the 1980s Lessing herself became a globetrotter, sometimes even travelling and speaking to support a new novel (see Chapters 7 and 8). Her travelling has taken her to Europe, Asia, Africa and North America and undoubtedly helped to increase her already large international audience. Critical commentary, once overwhelmingly American, now attracts other national scholars. That commentary suggests that Lessing is read differently in each country. In a critical climate that insists on the relativity of the text, these variations are compelling rather than confusing.

Lessing's current status as an international figure has yet to be adequately recognised and assessed, even by American critics who have written so much about her. It has come about fairly recently, in the early 1980s, and happens to have coincided with my tenure as editor of the *Doris Lessing Newsletter* (1982–8). Lessing's reputation abroad grew noticeably during those years, and the *DLN* overseas subscriber list reflected that growth. Then Jenny Taylor's *Notebooks/Memoirs/Archives* (1982) was published. It was the perfect catalyst. The resulting correspondence led to the broadening of Doris Lessing Modern Language Association sessions to include overseas scholars. Several issues of *DLN* were guest-edited by such scholars (Andrew Gurr from Britain; Eve Bertelsen from South Africa; Fernando Galván Reula from Spain). When I was asked to chair an MLA session, I had no hesitation in suggesting as a panel topic the international reception of Doris Lessing. The papers presented on that occasion, December 1986, were the precipitants for this volume. They were so good and so well received that a book about international reader response seemed their natural outgrowth. The essays by Clare Hanson, Nicole Ward Jouve and Eve Bertelsen and the comment on them by Ellen Cronan Rose demonstrated that such an enterprise did not have to be a mere compendium of statistics or a summary of trends as 'reception' studies once were. In fact, it validates and extends current critical theory about the relativity of the text and the nature of reader-response.

In these essays new critical evaluations are presented, at least one of which, Clare Hanson's, represents a radical rereading, in fact a rejection, of Lessing as a realistic novelist. Lessing's multiple texts multiply explosively beneath the special lenses of the different national readers. These national differences need to be seen and examined. *Le Carnet d'or* is, for example, central to the French reader, as *El Cuaderno dorado* is to the Spanish or *Ihr goldenes Notizbuch* is to the German; *The Golden Notebook* is 'unsatisfactory', even 'incoherent', to the South African reader, as Ellen Cronan Rose so effectively pointed out in her comments on the MLA papers. These divergent readings challenge readers and critics to create a critical approach to Lessing that is neither 'periscopic nor monoscopic' (Rose). The point is that comparing national responses opens a large and exciting window on the interaction between context and text.

It was inevitable that Lessing's 1960 title, *In Pursuit of the English*, would one day be turned around by critics to point at her. She has become our quarry, the object of our critical pursuit. Nine nations pursue her in this volume.[1] These nine, Zimbabwe, South Africa, England, the United States, Canada, France, Germany, Spain, the USSR, can be grouped in a number of ways. Grouping by language is one way to begin. In four of the nine, England, the US, South Africa and Zimbabwe, Lessing is read in English. In a fifth, officially bilingual Canada, Lessing's readers are probably in fact also English speaking. In four countries, France, Germany, Spain and the USSR, Lessing must be read largely in translation. In the two African countries, Zimbabwe and South Africa, Lessing's readership is probably largely white and English speaking, although the majority population is black and often multi-lingual. The two North American countries, Canada and the United States, have a colonial past which affects their present and which contains expected and unexpected analogues to white actions and responses in Rhodesia and South Africa. Canada also has an uneasy dependency relationship with the United States which Virginia Tiger's essay illuminates. Some would consider the two Germanies, East and West, dependencies of the USSR and the USA respectively. Thus, despite its non-colonial past, elements of contemporary German life have a colonial patina. As one would anticipate, Lessing's fortunes in East Germany and the USSR run a similar course. Franco's death in 1975 is causally related to the growth of Lessing's reception in Spain as *glasnost* may turn out to be in the USSR. Political configurations are, therefore, abundantly and inescapably related to literary judgements in these nine countries as they have been in Lessing's life and work. Political, Lessing's umbrella word for a long time, was once inextricably entwined for her with conditions/issues of gender, race and social policy.

Lessing may no longer use the 'political' in her old umbrella sense, but Africans white and black still do, as Anthony Chennells and Eve Bertelsen confirm. African Lessing, little known outside Africa, has a precise historical context, as Bertelsen points out. In the world of the small white elite, everyone knew one another. Responses to Lessing are therefore understandably frequently personal; she is the local girl who made good. Her radical politics gave her a kind of notoriety at home she never had in Europe. Headlines such as 'Doris Lessing Deserts the Veld for London' or 'Rhodesian Authoress Not Allowed to Enter SA' were not uncommon. Her stories and early novels were read as dangerous revisions of the typical white settler novel in their denial of the 'paradigm of white superiority and black inferiority' (see Anthony Chennells's essay).

Chennells forces us to see the incompleteness of this version of Lessing's Rhodesian stories. He digs deeper. Looking back on the stories from a Zimbabwean perspective permits him to read them as explorations of the 'contradictory themes within imperial discourse'. Those characters who escape settler racism and capitalism, typically children, outcasts, lonely prospectors or unsuccessful farmers like Dick Turner and Alfred Quest, do so within an ideology that is not Marxist but romantic anti-capitalism. Their escape is inevitably temporary or profoundly limited; 'adult discourse remains unaffected by these sudden surges of insight'. Chennells astutely recognises how alike are 'the epiphanies afforded by the veld' and those engendered by 'a man recovering his manhood in his encounter with the primitive'. (Although Chennells does not pursue the gender implications of this division, they are there.) The tensions in Lessing's stories clearly depend on a continual counterpoint 'between a romantic response to the African bush and the capitalism of the settlers which sought to transform it into profitable settlements, mining or agricultural land'.

Chennells's perspective undercuts those white romantic views of the land which Lessing's stories share: 'What to blacks was structured space was to the whites wilderness'. For blacks substitute Indians and you have the American pioneer ethos which has so many analogues to white African settler rationales. Settlers in both areas relied on force and occupation. Their descendants had the luxury of developing even more romantic attitudes towards the land which in the US were later elaborated and given mythic structure by novelists such as William Faulkner and Ernest Hemingway. Settlers never took African/Indian rights to their land seriously. In Africa, they always believed blacks could go back somewhere beyond the settlements, to some space 'which the settlers believed they should call home'. US settler beliefs were the same. The crucial difference between American blacks and African blacks, that the latter were in effect enslaved at home and the former taken from their homes and enslaved in another country, did not make for a different policy. In both countries, blacks were portable and treated as property.

Now that Zimbabwean discourse is black, Lessing's Rhodesian stories belong to the past. The *Encyclopedia Zimbabwe* entry on Doris

Lessing that frames Chennells's essay tends to marginalise her because she is white; for the present, Zimbabweans must 'write white authors as peripheral'. Zimbabwean cultural nationalism has many historical precedents, especially in nations formerly colonial. Consider Herman Melville's classic essay on Nathaniel Hawthorne in which he enjoins Americans to praise American literature over English literature even when it is mediocre. Independence has made it possible for Africans to take a similar position and to insist on controlling their own discourses. Moses, the necessarily silent figure in Lessing's first novel, *The Grass Is Singing* (1950), is no longer silent or in the background. Even a person so critical of white mores as Martha Quest does not realise for a long time that from the British point of view blacks have no history before colonialism. Martha cannot find a single book about the black historical past when she tries to organise a class for blacks about blacks (*A Ripple from the Storm*, [1958])[2] From the British point of view, African history began with their arrival. A similar bias is imbedded in the Columbus-discovered-America ritual fact in every American child's history book, for the Europeans discovered an America long known to the Indians by other names. Lessing responds to the bias imbedded in place names by changing the name of her fictional locale from the English-imposed Southern Rhodesia (after Cecil Rhodes) in *The Grass Is Singing* to the African Zambesia in the Martha Quest novels. That change metaphorically denies white appropriation of the land and returns it to its owners.

Eve Bertelsen (Chapter 2) speaks as much for her region, Southern Africa, as she does for her country, South Africa. She spells out what is demonstrated throughout this volume, that an awareness of the interaction between context and text 'calls into question generalisations regarding the "universal" significance and quality' of Lessing's work. Lessing's reputation in South Africa, based on *Grass*, the Rhodesian stories, the first three Martha Quest novels, *Retreat to Innocence* and *In Pursuit of the English*, was at its peak in the 1950s. (It did not rise with *The Golden Notebook* [1962] as it did in the US and on the Continent.) For in the 1950s, Lessing spoke directly to her primarily white African reader. Her private and artistic imperatives coincided with the political imperatives of South African life and made her work seem, for a brief period, 'urgent, compelling, and personally relevant' to South Africans. As these imperatives diverged, Lessing's reputation declined.

One example of Lessing's always 'impeccable' use of history, to use Chennells's word, is her citing of the postwar events that moved South Africa further right politically. Postwar disillusion permeates *Landlocked* (1965). Thomas Stern, alone within Martha Quest's left group, has the insight and the courage to predict a 'Nats' (Nationalist) victory in South Africa. That victory in 1948 represents for Bertelsen 'a coercive rewriting of the informal racism of colonial times'. The primary political problems of the period – racism, threats to white supremacy and the resultant personal dilemmas for whites – are all written into Lessing's fictions. When Lessing leaves her African locale in *The Four-Gated City* (1969), she has already moved far into the inner space that has since preoccupied her. In a turnabout, the revolution that Lessing had abandoned as 'a lost cause' in the 1950s became a central fact of South African life. Lessing's developing 'contempt for politics and her exclusive concentration on individual interiority' struck the South African reader as 'bizarre', for 'everything in South Africa is political and the reception of Lessing particularly so'. In a country in which urban terrorism is a serious political option, Lessing's *The Good Terrorist* seems trivial, even opportunistic. It could be cynically described as 'yet another' exploitation of a ' "cash-crop" theme'.

In Africa Lessing felt herself an outsider as white, female and Red. In England Lessing added colonial to her outsider inscriptions. These outsider states did not, however, in Clare Hanson's judgement, inhibit a positive critical reception so long as Lessing's work was perceived as realist. This is precisely the point at which Hanson's reading of Lessing is so radical. Hanson (Chapter 3) charges that the English 'misreading' determines the positive reception of *The Grass Is Singing* (described as 'ecstatic') and explains why Lessing's reputation has been 'downhill all the way' since then. Even *The Golden Notebook* was not positively received; as one reviewer put it, 'there is no breaking of forms [in it], but an inability to impose form at all'. Hanson's provocative position is that Lessing has never been the kind of realist she describes in 'The Small Personal Voice' and that the essay is itself 'a piece of camouflage' related to the kind of camouflage the pseudonymous Jane Somers much later provided. This position erodes other received opinions about Lessing, especially the widely held one that Lessing has no style.

The question of style/medium is central. For Hanson, it allies Lessing to post-modernists who are 'obsessed by . . . the falsity' of their medium. She notes Lessing's 'wide range of styles' which shift 'from, for example, the register of documentary to that of romantic fiction to that of social satire'. The English have been blind and deaf to this range, unaware of Lessing's 'acute sense of the relativity of style'. This unawareness ensured that a novel like *The Good Terrorist* would be misunderstood. Hanson rejects a reading that endorses 'the clichés of suburban fascism' embodied in the ex-radical mother figure, invariably taken as a stand-in for her author. She argues instead that the 'grey and textureless language' is deliberate, not lazy, and intended to define the inner life of the novel.

Where do English feminists stand on these issues? Those who had read Lessing empathetically, fervently, often in tandem with Simone de Beauvoir's *The Second Sex* (e.g. Wilson), have turned away from her. The feminist movement, reflecting the larger English resistance to experiment, cannot put aside 'its deep-rooted mistrust of any departure from the Marxist–feminist model of women's oppression'. As a result, English feminists 'have missed out, most crucially, on what Lessing has been trying to do with gender and gender-expectations in her space fiction'. As an example of Lessing's 'play' with gender, Hanson cites *The Marriages Between Zones Three, Four, and Five.* That novel, mistakenly read by some readers in England as a celebration of gender roles as we know them, in fact moves 'beyond gender difference' if not beyond 'difference itself'.

Hanson's daring rereading of Lessing defines her as a fully post-modern and post-humanist writer who 'challenges both the authority of identity and the identity of the author'. Lessing is, for Hanson, a writer who should be read in the context of theorists like Julia Kristeva and Jacques Derrida. This provocative position is slowly beginning to revise Lessing criticism (e.g. Schweickart, Hite, Draine and Barzilai). It certainly places Lessing where she belongs, in 'the international, transcultural marketplace'. But in her move 'beyond bourgeois humanism and contemporary sexual politics', Lessing seems to have, in Hanson's witty phrasing, 'outdistanced the English of whom she once, disingenuously, declared herself to be in pursuit'. It has also scuttled her two primary audiences in England, the realist and the feminist.

The United States's reception of Lessing is tied squarely to the women's movement, which is itself historically and ideologically tied to the civil rights and anti-Vietnam-War movements of the late 1960s, as Ellen Rose's essay so meticulously documents (see

Chapter 4). The American Lessing is a women's movement author, even when women identify severe limitations in Lessing's depictions of them. In fact, women critics have been more generous to Lessing than she has been to them. She denies the women's movement the variety and complexity it has in sideswipes like the one in 'The Small Personal Voice' about the use of 'the sex war as a serious substitute for social struggle'.

The American Lessing, born in response to *The Golden Notebook*, tends not to be African at all but cosmopolitan, urban, professional and woman-centred. The local habitation and a name that so interested African readers gets whited out in US Lessing criticism, which begins where African and English readings had more or less stopped. This erasure of African Lessing has its special ironies since it occurred in a context of the 1960s and 1970s that claimed concern for the civil rights of American Blacks.[3] Annis Pratt confirms that by the end of the 1960s *The Golden Notebook* 'had been appropriated by many feminists as "a document in the history of liberation"' (see Chapter 4). The anti-war and women's movements, it must be underscored, 'assumed their characteristic shape in the university'. The university was, for a while, capable of acting politically in ways that affected national policy. The trajectory of Lessing's reputation is intimately related to that special moment. Rose's decision to choose the moment when Lessing stormed the university through its marginal women, minorities and radicals plays out the growth of Lessing's reputation in the academy, one dependent on the growing influence of feminist critics. Thus, Lessing's reception in the US becomes 'a paradigm of feminism's relationship to the academy from the early seventies to the present'.

The Lessing of the 1960s and early 1970s spoke to women hungry to 'know how to behave, what to hope to be like', what Virginia Tiger identifies as the 'Lessing changed my life' cry. For them Anna Wulf was a real woman. Women needed to see their images in literature, needed to have their experiences validated. In courses, books, articles and MLA symposia, Lessing criticism flourished and Lessing seemed to be close to making a place for herself in a new canon. 'But,' in Rose's words, 'a funny thing happened on the way to the canon. Doris Lessing stopped writing meaningfully for the general public' – and presumably for women. In that moment of coincidence and collaboration in US cultural history, when a generation of activists attempted to reformulate the canon, 'the distinction between the general or common reader and the academic' one was blurred (letter, Rose to Sprague, 18 July 1988). *The Golden Notebook* seemed written for the occasion. But the occasion was fleeting. In Rose's judgement, Lessing is now 'largely . . . the property of academics' (letter, Rose to Sprague, 18 July 1988) and feminist critics have shifted their theoretical ground, as has criticism in general, to post-structuralism. Their 'post-feminist' students, who are likely to find Lessing dated, may, however, be in for a surprise, for, in Rose's arresting image, '*The Golden Notebook* is ticking like a time bomb on college syllabi all over the USA'.

Canada's reading of Lessing in no way reflects the country's long-enduring double status as a cultural dependent of two colossi, England and the United States. That reading, totally independent in a number of striking ways, begins, appropriately and uniquely enough, with *In Pursuit of the English*, whose title evokes the historic quest of English-descended Canadians and the more recent one 'undertaken . . . by every aspiring Canadian novelist' (Chapter 5). That supposed centrepiece of the Lessing canon, *The Golden Notebook*, was apparently ignored in Canada whose more sustained interest in Lessing was to coincide with its own cultural renaissance. Virginia Tiger places that renaissance in 1973 when cultural nationalism and the new feminism 'charged' and shaped the new 'intellectual exuberance' of the country. Tiger's reading is the first to align Lessing's reputation with the appearance of a clutch of new novelists, Margaret Laurence and Margaret Atwood among them. These novelists were responsible for the second stage of the Canadian reading of Lessing, those 'woman-centred exegeses' which followed the themes of 'exilic colonialism' found in *In Pursuit*.

Tiger, who locates the third phase of the Canadian reading of Lessing in Margaret Atwood's *Survival*, cogently ties the positive Canadian reading of the later Lessing novels to their emphatic survival theme. Thus, while so many readers – and nations – have turned away from the *Canopus* novels, Canada has found something of itself in them. The Canadian readings of *Memoirs of a Survivor* as well as the *Canopus* novels represent a complex mirroring process. *The Making of the Representative for Planet 8*, set on a planet dying of a glacial invasion, perhaps most reflects Canadian geographical realities and myths, 'matching', as it does, 'the Canadian archetypal experience of seige'. By its climate and land, Canada seems always to have been enjoined, like the Planet 8 population, 'to forge communal resources for survival'. Tiger sees the likeness between two distant and apparently dissimilar vastnesses, the African veld and the Canadian wilderness: 'Like Africa, Canada strands individuals in vast territories'.

In the countries so far discussed Lessing could reach most of her readers without the intervention of translations or time distortions. Her publishing history in France, Germany, Spain and the USSR is the most quantifiable example of context affecting text. Nicole Ward Jouve (Chapter 6) notes the appearance of Lessing's work 'in perfect disregard of chronology'; Fernando Galván Reula (Chapter 8) similarly notes 'the chaotic chronology of the transla-tions' in Spain. In Germany, translations of the *Children of Violence* series overlapped with those of the *Canopus in Argos* series, as Mona Knapp reports. The book that initiated Lessing's reputation in Canada, *In Pursuit of the English* (1960), appeared in 1986 in Germany at the same time as the 1985 volume *The Good Terrorist*. In France, four Lessing works appeared in one year and the Martha Quest novels caused some confusion because they seemed to have been written after *The Golden Notebook*. Jouve's judgement that the French chronology, because it 'miniaturises and deforms the English publishing time', and thereby erases 'writing as process and progress', applies equally well to the German, Spanish and Russian chronologies. The Soviet chronology is unique, as Lorna Peterson has discovered for us despite significant archival limi-tations; in that country Lessing was erased for twenty years (1957–77) before her presence was even lightly redrawn.

Politics interact with text in these countries as well. There are, for example, two Lessings in Germany, one West German, the other East German. In West Germany Lessing's reputation was inhibited in part because she was a communist; in East Germany and the USSR she was first noticed because she was a communist, then ignored because she wasn't. International feminism, a power-ful political phenomenon, is directly responsible for the runaway success of *The Golden Notebook* in France and Germany, according to Jouve and Knapp. *The Golden Notebook* was also a smashing success in Spain – in fact, Galván thinks Lessing is, for the Spanish reading public, a one-book author – but less because of international feminism than because Spain was so open to foreign influence after Franco's death in 1975. It is still a striking fact that it took fourteen years for *Le Carnet d'or* (1976) and sixteen for its German and Spanish equivalents to appear. This delay makes the Russian gap seem somewhat less gargantuan, for so far as Peterson has been able to discover, *The Golden Notebook* has yet to be translated in the Soviet Union. By now, Lessing's novels are appearing regularly and in chronological order in Western Europe, although not in Eastern Europe.

The explosion of Lessing's reputation in the 1980s in these countries, the result of complex political and sociological factors, proceeded with Lessing's active support. She travelled to Germany in 1981 and 1986, to France in 1981 and 1984–5, and to Spain in 1983 and 1987. She also visited other countries in Europe, North America and Asia during this period and, in the process, became a collaborator in the media process she has so often scolded. Her only other voyage as a writer was undertaken long before, in 1952, when she travelled to the Soviet Union as a member of a writer's group. She was then part of the socialist 'we', not of the Sufi 'we'. Neither 'we' has inhibited Lessing's very outspoken 'I' self.

The early 1980s may remain the high point of Lessing's fortunes in Europe, for these fortunes have already begun a shift that may turn out to be seismic. In West Germany, the feminist journal *Emma* (the name has ironic echoes for Lessing-watchers; Jane Somers in *The Diary of a Good Neighbour* almost changes the title of her magazine from the radical, exotic *Lilith* to *Martha*, a serviceable household name more like *Emma*) harshly attacked *The Good Terrorist* for its reductive view of left politics. In France, to adopt Jouve's gold metaphor, the 'Nobélisable' gold standard set in *Le Carnet d'or* may be undergoing some erosion, as it is in Spain where the feminist writer Carmen Martín Gaite called *A Proper Marriage* (translated in 1979–80) a classic example of 'the dangers of dogmatism', a statement she might not have made the year the novel was published (1954).

Lessing's relationship with the Soviet Union is special, not because its readings of her work are unexpected, but because Lessing and her major centres of consciousness, Martha Quest and Anna Wulf, construct a USSR as mythic in its lineaments as the England colonials pursued. How Lessing reads these two countries into her fictions has an interest surely greater than how they read her. In *A Ripple from the Storm* and *Landlocked* Martha Quest dreams about both countries; the USSR dominates her thoughts during wartime (the storm in the title of *Ripple* refers to the fighting on the Eastern Front); England appears to be a homeland, the country Martha dreams of moving to after the war. The USSR is also a homeland, the homeland of the socialism Martha Quest and Anna Wulf and her creator espoused. (Russia may also share literary homeland status with England, for if we take 'The Small Personal Voice' and the 1971 preface to *The Golden Notebook* at their word, Tolstoy is the writer Lessing most wanted to emulate.) The death of the dream of socialism represents a major trauma for Anna Wulf. The living Lessing and her authorial voice in the Martha/Anna novels relate to Russia in complex imaginative and psychological ways. Both socialist Russia and mother England are fiery presences in Lessing's life and in her fictional structures.

The official Soviet Lessing is a most shorn and diminished creature constructed largely of Lessing's African stories, *Martha Quest*, two post-1950s works and a blank where *The Golden Notebook* ought to be. It is a Lessing more rigorously limited to the 1950s than the Southern African Lessing. There is, however, an interesting coincidence, for in both Southern Africa and the USSR, Lessing is wholly African, a writer praised for her African subject-matter and ignored or criticised when she leaves it. The Soviet focus was underlined in 1980 when *The Grass Is Singing* was translated in honour of Zimbabwean independence. The thirty-year delay both validates and undercuts the Soviet African bias; *Grass* was translated, not *The Golden Notebook*, but so belatedly that it exposes limits to the bias. The more common Euro-American focus on the English Lessing has its own obvious limitations.

The words on her page have not changed, but our perceptions of them have. Once Lessing was autobiographical and realist or political and feminocentric if not feminist; once she was an admirer of certain kinds of madness, once she had no style, once she was a communist; now she is a post-modernist and a post-humanist who has appreciated and demonstrated the relativity of style. She has also been called neo-conservative. The Canadian critic who described her *Canopus* volumes as 'Star Wars for the intellectuals' (see Chapter 5) wittily phrased a common conception of the ideology of these volumes. The Lessing who complains loudly about the critics who stuff her into neatly labelled little boxes calls herself a Sufi. But she may slip out of that box (for the time being perceived as capacious) when we least expect her to. Her next departure, if there is one, is likely to seem opportunistic to some, prescient or canny to others.

Lessing's international, transcultural qualities are differently situated. They are too deeply imbedded to fluctuate with any market or fashion. Implacably present in her work, permanently imprinted as it were, they can have a transforming power in many areas. The university curriculum is one. Lessing's example can show us 'how un-English English literature is' (Dasenbrock, p. 58). What is one to do, asks an American professor, with writers like Lessing, V. S. Naipaul and Salman Rushdie? He argues that they belong in 'a reconstructed English curriculum that [has] escaped the prison of English and American literature and . . . moved toward a global awarensss of literature in English' (Dasenbrock, p. 58). Perhaps feminist readings of Lessing's fictions will fuse with transcultural readings to give us new readings of Lessing's always prickly forays into territories familiar and unfamiliar. Our efforts may, in the process, help to loosen the national biases reflected in our school curricula.

Contextual readings neither impoverish nor fragment Lessing's work, as this collection shows. They refuse to denude Lessing of her rich political matter, or to validate a simplistic mirroring approach to it or to her entire corpus. They lead, in fact, to new ways of seeing, here, for example, to the variety of ways in which particular cultural nationalisms have appropriated Lessing. Are all these readings partial? Undoubtedly, but partial readings are a permanent and not necessarily unwelcome part of critical realities. The nine readings presented in this collection are neither adulatory nor unanimous. They continue to raise major questions about Lessing, including the long-standing one about her effectiveness as a writer. Is her work, to use Jouve's phrasing, the result of 'an unsolved aesthetic problem' or a 'chosen' strategy, 'a post-modernist device' (Chapter 6)? There is no consensus on this question. The crucial issues may be better served by a different formulation, one that Rose and Peterson, favour. They prefer to apply Charles Watkin's insistence in *Briefing for a Descent into Hell* on the principle of 'and, and, and' over the dichotomous and limiting 'either/or'.

Lessing is, of course, still in the world. In fact, she has never left it. Her practical eye keeps her mystical eye in line. She cannot, like one of her early heroines, Julia Barr, 'retreat to innocence'. The 'shock of recognition' she long ago triggered continues to reverberate in our consciousness.[4] Women have felt that shock, so have men, so have third-world peoples, so have all readers who want to test, stretch or break through the boundaries of accepted political, social, psychological and artistic thought and practice.

To examine Lessing's world-wide reception is to examine the commonalities and the differences that at once divide and join our world. At the very least, these varied readings force us to re-examine the meaning of universality. They also remind us of the double lens that keeps Lessing both in and out of the world, for Lessing remains intransigently what the French call *engagée*, fully 'in the world' even when she seems most out of it.

Notes

1. Dee Seligman is, to my knowledge, the first to have used the title 'In Pursuit of the Doris Lessing' in print. It was as irresistibly apt for her biographical pursuit as it is for the critical, socio-cultural–political pursuits of this volume.

   I regret that my efforts to secure an Argentinian or other Latin American contributor were unsuccessful. (Lessing's stories were recently on the bestseller list in Argentina.) I wish especially to thank Olga Kattan, Edith Grossman, Luisa Valenzuela and Rolando Costa Picazo for their efforts to help me. I can report that Costa Picazo was in the presence of translating *The Fifth Child* during our correspondence (1988).

2. For an extended discussion of this generally undervalued novel, see Sprague, Chapter 7.

3. I am indebted to Lorna Peterson for urging me to highlight this anachoronism (letter to the author, 11 August 1988). Some critics have noted the limited presence of race and class in the American construction of Lessing (Bertelsen) and its noticeably Jungian tilt (Sprague and Tiger).

4. Herman Melville's phrase has entered common literary parlance. It occurs in his essay 'Hawthorne and his Mosses' (1850).

Works Cited

Barzilai, Shuli. 'Unmaking the Words That Make Us: Doris Lessing's "How I Finally Lost My Heart"', *Style* 22.4 (Winter 1988): 595–611.

Bertelsen, Eve, ed. Introduction, *Doris Lessing*. Johannesburg: McGraw Hill, 1985. 15–28.

Dasenbrock, Reed Way. 'English Department Geography'. *Profession 87* (1987): 53–9.

Draine, Betsy. *Substance under Pressure: Artistic Coherence and Evolving Form.* Madison: University of Wisconsin Press, 1983.

Hite, Molly. '(En)Gendering Metafiction: Women Writers, Experimental Narrative, and Doris Lessing's *The Golden Notebook*'. Unpublished paper presented at MLA, 1986.

Lessing, Doris. 'In the World, Not of It' (1971), *A Small Personal Voice*. Ed. Paul Schlueter. New York: Knopf/Vintage, 1975. 129–37.

——, 'The Small Personal Voice' (1957), *A Small Personal Voice*. Ed. Paul Schlueter. New York: Knopf/Vintage, 1975. 3–21.

Rose, Ellen. 'A Response to Papers by Eve Bertelsen, Nicole Ward Jouve and Clare Hanson'. Unpublished MLA Response, 1986.

Schweickart, Patrocinio. 'Reading a Wordless Statement: The Structure of *The Golden Notebook*'. *Modern Fiction Studies* 31.2 (Summer 1985): 263–79.

Sprague, Claire. *Rereading Doris Lessing: Narrative Strategies of Doubling and Repetition*. Chapel Hill, NC: University of North Carolina Press, 1987.

Sprague, Claire, and Virginia Tiger, eds. Introduction *Critical Essays on Doris Lessing*. Boston, Mass.: G. K. Hall, 1986. 1–26.

Taylor, Jenny, ed. *Notebooks/Memoirs/Archives: Reading and Rereading Doris Lessing*. London: Routledge & Kegan Paul, 1982.

Wilson, Elizabeth. 'Yesterday's Heroines: On Rereading Lessing and de Beauvoir'. *Notebooks/Memoirs/Archives: Reading and Rereading Doris Lessing*. Ed. Jenny Taylor. London: Routledge & Kegan Paul, 1982. 57–74.

1

Reading Doris Lessing's Rhodesian Stories in Zimbabwe

ANTHONY CHENNELLS

In the new *Tabex Encyclopedia Zimbabwe* (1987) Doris Lessing is awarded a place in the canon of Zimbabwean writers not because of her merits as a writer, nor because of her reception by Zimbabweans, but because of the way she was read by her fellow settlers. She and Arthur Shearly Cripps are singled out for their opposition to the racial policies of colonial governments which 'led to their both being viewed in an unfavourable light by the local white community' (p. 219). That she is mentioned at all is obviously a concession. Zimbabwean literature is defined as 'the works of Zimbabwean Africans who through their prose and poetry have expressed the human and cultural aspirations of the nation and its people' (p. 219). Such a definition disqualifies Lessing on two grounds. Not only is she white but almost invariably in her writing blacks either look back to tradition and the past with nostalgia or aspire, not to a new nationhood, but to a more central place in the settler society which had marginalised them for so many years. What the *Encyclopedia*'s entry does do by including Lessing and Cripps is recognise that the liberal narratives of a few writers subverted the dominant discourse of settler novelists. That discourse wrote Africa 'as a primitive continent and a place of adventure, with African nationalism as a threat to the colonial status quo' (p. 219). By refusing to deal in such stereotypes, liberal novelists, the entry seems to imply, created a literary space within which African novelists could work and from which they could address the real issues that one day would make up the Zimbabwean identity. If settlers regarded Lessing and Cripps with hostility, it was because they recognised that both they and the blacks were being written in a way that denied the paradigm of

17

white superiority and black inferiority which is the basic structural model of so much of their writing.

The *Encyclopedia* entry is a good example of cultural nationalism as an important theme in contemporary Zimbabwean literary discourse. In the very terms in which it produces itself, cultural nationalism in Zimbabwe has to write white authors as peripheral and, where it praises them, does so in terms of their necessarily small contribution to nationalism. It is satisfied in short when it has identified their political stance in relation to nationalism. Nationalism is of its very nature inward-looking, and cultural nationalism is unlikely to be either precise about or generous towards the discourses which it has replaced. Not only does it run the risk of attributing to settler writing fixed discourses which are seen to remain intact during ninety years of settler rule, but it also foregrounds the presence and absence of black nationalism in those settler discourses, when for much of Rhodesia's history, the settlers saw nationalism as something which belonged to the past, not to the future. In fact the settler novelists, with a few exceptions, stopped writing Rhodesia as a locale for savagery and adventure in the early years of the century and as soon as the threat of another uprising had become sufficiently remote. As Rhodesia became familiar to its settlers its metonymies were more likely to be dust, drought and disillusionment than 'witch-doctors', warriors and white heroism. Occasionally the poverty and tedium of rural life might be spiced with fantasies of savage blacks and 'another rising', but as Lessing herself shows in *The Glass Is Singing* and other works, these were more in the nature of communal neurosis than a deeply held conviction of a probable political development. The authors, singled out by the *Encyclopedia*'s entry as particularly guilty of reinforcing the stereotypes of primitive Africa, are authors of the 1960s and 1970s,[1] writing when African nationalism had become more militant and its militancy more effective. Settler novelists resuscitated the old images of primitive Africa at that moment when the secondary resistance movements started to organise themselves as modern guerilla armies. The Rhodesian context in which Lessing lived – the 1920s, 1930s and 1940s – were the very years in which whites were most at liberty to create a discourse of Rhodesia of which they were the subjects and blacks were contemptuously objectified not as savages but as backward, superstitious, irritating and harmless. *The Grass Is Singing* was felt to be so objectionable by the settlers because, despite Moses's silence, his actions show that he has written himself as subject of an alternative discourse. The conspiratorial silence with which the Turners' neighbours greet Mary's murder and which is broken only by a few tentative and unsuccessful attempts to recover the dominant discourse (Moses knows that he has laid his hands on one of the king's women for example) is a necessary silence. In their refusal to question the events leading up to the murder, the settlers are refusing to confront the very contradictions which their racist ideology is designed to conceal. Fifteen years after *The Grass Is Singing* was published, when Wilbur Smith was beginning his prolific career, such evasion was no longer possible. The nationalists were recruiting young people for training and the settler attempt to retain control of their destiny by declaring themselves unilaterally independent of Britain was shown to be a futile gesture as sporadic violence spread into nationwide war. However whites were going to write nationalist militancy – and it was in fact written as savagery – it could not be absorbed into silence. The very stridency of the alternative discourse made that impossible.

The magnitude of the changes in Rhodesia from the early 1960s to 1980, when Zimbabwe became independent, does create problems for Lessing's Zimbabwean critics. Those turbulent twenty years, which turned upside down the settler world she knew so well, quite literally created a new country. The instincts of the writer of the *Encyclopedia* entry are sound enough when it is implied that, in terms of contemporary Zimbabwean literature, Lessing's importance is principally historical. She and Cripps represent those maverick voices which remind us that white Rhodesia was not so overwhelmingly committed to a single racist discourse as some of the new Zimbabwean historiography seems to maintain. But it cannot be emphasised strongly enough that even the discourse of the liberal voices is no longer possible. Almost invariably they assume the permanence of white political control and the muted hints that one day blacks will reassume the direction of their lives refers to a day so distanced from the present as to become mere utopianism.

What then is the feature of Zimbabwean writing which seems to date Lessing's work when it is read in a Zimbabwean context? It is primarily the attempt by black Zimbabweans to regain or assume control of a literary discourse that was dominated for ninety years by settler or metropolitian models. Zimbabweans will produce Zimbabwean subjects of Zimbabwean discourses. A similar inten-

tion can be seen in historical writing. Only in the last twenty years
has there been a sustained attempt to write African history with
Africans rather than imperialists as agents of historical processes.
Africa's history, like any continent's history, has to be measured
in millennia rather than centuries and as such it is not the product
of imperialism. Even during the imperial epoch, when Africans
could do no more than respond to imperial initiatives, there was
an African discourse which shaped that response and which
imperial historians largely ignored. Modern African historians are
only now in the process of recovering that silenced discourse. It is
not surprising then that the first novel written in English by a
black Zimbabwean – Stanlake Samkange's *On Trial for My Country*,
which was first published in 1966 – should be a historical novel
and centre on the negotiations which preceded the occupation of
the country by the first settlers. Nor is it surprising, given that
early date and the conservatism of the author that the trial of the
novel's title should have two accused: Cecil Rhodes, the imperialist,
whose machinations gained the country for his company and for
Britain, and Lobengula, the Ndebele king, whose vacillations made
Rhodesia's grab for the north a great deal easier than it might have
been. When it was written the 'My Country' of the title was an
acknowledgement that both black and white had a right to call the
country theirs even while the 'Trial' uncovered the combination of
chicanery and weakness which had given the whites that right.
When we read it now, the novel seems to bend over backwards to
avoid offending the whites – it did offend them and the book was
banned – but its importance lies in the fact that it is a text which
produces a Lobengula who has a case and argues it with dignity
and force. In the articulate Lobengula of the novel we have already
been shifted a long way from Moses's silent endurance.

In 1975, Samkange's *The Mourned One* showed how far the
literary discourses of black Zimbabweans had changed. Here twins
are born to a rural woman at a time when custom demanded that
twins were killed at birth. A missionary's intervention saves the
twins and one is left in his rural and traditional home while the
other is raised at a mission station with all the advantages that a
white child would have. Only when he leaves the mission and
tries to make his way in the larger racist society does Muchemwa
have to confront the implications of what it means to be black in
the segregated Rhodesia of the 1930s.

He finds refuge in another mission where a trumped-up charge of rape is brought against him; he is found guilty and condemned to death. His last speech is addressed to his brother whom, over the years, he has come to envy. Zana may have the limited horizon of a traditional upbringing but he has been spared the worries that knowledge of a larger and more complex world would necessarily expose him to. He has not been exposed to the insults of whites, which Muchemwa has had to endure through his knowledge of English. Muchemwa's exposure to settler society has made him realise that:

> There are many things in African culture that are superior to European ways. We must not lose them for the sake of turning ourselves into black white men. 'Fools are the tools of the wise,' the white man says. 'Let Africans sleep so that we can use them.'   (pp. 144–6)

Muchemwa goes on to proclaim:

> Education will ultimately enable us to meet the white man on his own ground and topple him from his pedestal. Sons of Africa will, one day, arise and recover the rule of our land from the white man. They will do this, Gushunyo, because the white man is rejecting brotherhood with the black man. If I hang and die, the brotherhood of man, peace and racial harmony in this land will die with me; because when the white man rejects me – one, who except for the colour of his skin, is a European – black men everywhere will realise that there can be no half measures, that co-operation with these people is impossible and that either the white man or the black man must rule this country but not both.   (pp. 144–6)

The contradictions in that speech are revealing. Muchemwa envies Zana because the very limitations or rural life have allowed him to concentrate on that instinctive respect for other people's humanity which African society induces in and demands of its members. At the same time Muchemwa argues that only Western education will enable the African to confront the white man on his own ground. Elsewhere in Africa that nostalgia for an African past untouched by the West manifests itself in the negritude movement. By 1975 negritude was generally seen as too defensive and impractical in Southern and East Africa where more complex responses were required to confront colonialism's and neo-colonialism's denigration of African culture and the African past. The confusions of Samkange's narrator can thus be read as expressions of the very different discourses of the 1930s and the 1970s. The comforting limitations of tradition, complacent at its very inability to change, belong to the 1930s; the rejection of half measures and of power sharing and the affirmation of black rule belongs to the 1970s. What is valuable in African culture will be preserved by African governments whose members have been educated along Western lines. In 1975 with most of Africa freed from imperial and settler control such a strategy was no longer utopian.

In 1978 Samkange published his third novel, *Year of the Uprising*, which deals with the *Chimurenga* of 1896 and 1897. The fact that this primary resistance movement was crushed completely is less important in the novel than those signs within the nationalist discourse which signified the traditional unity of the people and their determination to throw over settler rule. Within the novel the people of Zimbabwe are linked by a common religion which transcends regional rivalries and which inspires them to rise against the invader. Great Zimbabwe is made the ancient political and religious centre for the entire land and it is there that the insurrectionist chiefs gather to plot the strategies of the rising. Most of these details belong to a nationalist history of the 1960s and had been refuted when the book was written. But in 1978, shortly before the Geneva conference of Zimbabwean independence, its very distortions of history allow it to draw into a single discourse the Zimbabwean past, the primary resistance struggle, the liberation war, which was then being waged, and Zimbabwe as a nation.

Samkange is a minor talent. A historian by profession, his novels often reveal the problems that he has in shifting from history into myth in order not to subvert the certainties of his own polemic. The shifts of emphasis in his writings are, however, symptomatic of the shifts within the nationalist discourse during the twenty years before Zimbabwean independence.

In any racially segrated society, the discrete spaces which the races occupy assume a central significance in defining both political and personal relationships. The division of Rhodesian into black and white areas, location and suburb, farm and reserve, structures the landscape of the novels of many black Zimbabweans. Both in Shona and English novels, the towns in particular are read as hostile, alien and yet for some a seductive space. Kizito Muchemwa has spoken of the urban areas as places where before independence blacks were unwelcome and temporary sojourners (p. vi). George Kahari (1986), writing of the ways in which the towns are seen in the Shona novel, says: 'The urban areas in . . . these stories . . . are soul-destructive, destroying such things as human relationships and such values as hospitality. The urban areas are melting pots in which "things fall apart"' – (p. 107). The most powerful novel in English by a black Zimbabwean is Charles Mungoshi's *Waiting for the Rain*, published in 1975. Although the setting is entirely within a Tribal Trust Land,[2] both the adjoining white farms and the distant city exists in the consciousness of the characters as alternative space liable to draw young people from family and ancestors. Some of the power of the novel derives from Mungoshi's use of multiple discourses which confront the complexities of Zimbabwe in a way no other Zimbabwean using English as his or her medium has done. One of the discourses is produced by the town-educated Lucifer, who is sceptical of the loyalties demanded of him by family rituals and the ancestors around whom such rituals cluster. His discourse is in effect an anti-pastoral, a mode rare in African writing where the nostalgia of a novel like *Things Fall Apart* has had a profound effect on the literary imagination. Lucifer thinks of the rural areas as 'the failure's junk-heap . . . where you come back to die, having lived all your life elsewhere'.

> When in the city, people talk of home, he feels his lack and wants to hide. For them, home is where dreams and innocence still survive. For them, it is the place to go to when they are tired of the city – the city, an alien place that only jangles to the tune of coins. Home is where Father, Mother, Brother and Sister are. But for Lucifer . . . At home, the worms set to work on you the day you are conceived. And home is where the rain comes late, if it does come at all, and the animals simply drop dead and the old folks are abandoned to wait the black messiah with a curse on their twisted lips.   (Mungoshi, pp. 162–3)

Lucifer's cynicism is countered by the alternative discourse of those members of his family who cling to tradition. His grandfather makes drums, musical instruments that are a central feature of rituals where communication with the ancestors is established. Even this pious activity is viewed ironically in Lucifer's discourse.

The cutting down of trees has already desertified the land. In making the ritual instruments which maintain a continuity between those who are living and those who have gone before, the very land itself will become too barren to support the community's continued existence. Very soon the people will have to go and find somewhere else to live. 'Already some of them, those less attached to roots and family and "our ancestors" are moving out' (p. 162). Lucifer may subvert the discourse of the traditionalists but he himself is not a free agent. According to the traditional discourse the whole family carries the burden of a restless ancestor who was not restored to the earth with appropriate rituals. In his very anxiety to escape from a home which he writes as narrow, prejudiced and occasionally brutal, Lucifer may be responding to the urgings of that unquiet spirit. The traditional discourse maintains that his attempt to escape will be as doomed as was that of his ancestor. *Waiting for the Rain* is open-ended. The discourses which have ironically commented upon one another throughout the novel refuse closure. The metonymies which could extend either the traditional or the modern discourse are metonymies which will be written only within the historical processes which transformed Rhodesia into Zimbabwe and consolidated the independence of the new nation. They will be extended only by the degree of emphasis Zimbabweans choose to place on traditional culture.

The transformation of Rhodesia into Zimbabwe is the most fundamental spatial transformation which our literature has had to confront. As Mungoshi's novel suggests, however, there is no guarantee that one or other of his discourses will prevail in the new state. For some commentators Zimbabwe has more resolutely turned its back on the traditional discourse than the African rural areas of Rhodesia ever allowed themselves to do. These look at the new black elites whom they claim have simply accepted the ideologies of white Rhodesia. For others, like Samkange, the mere fact that blacks control the government and thus the public discourse is a guarantee that Zimbabwean discourse will prevail, aware of its roots, and yet inscribed by the developments within the new state. For these, Rhodesia and the ideologies of Rhodesia are written out of the discourse.

I would identify with the second group. The first group argues that a bourgeoisie is a bourgeoisie whether it is black or white, a point of view which seems to be unacceptably reductionist. The distinctive character of white Rhodesia had its basis in the fact that it was a white community, numerically outnumbered by vast numbers of blacks and constantly defining itself in the differences it believed existed between it and them. As important as this was white Rhodesia's attitude to the land itself. What Africans saw as places crowded with ancestral associations and spiritual presences, the whites saw as empty spaces waiting to be shaped by their creative will. What to blacks was structured space was to the whites wilderness. No black can read Zimbabwe as the settlers read the Rhodesian bush. Whatever class divisions exist in Zimbabwe (and they are real enough), they are class divisions among blacks and not the racial divisions of the past. Zimbabwean blacks are people who have inherited the land; the settlers were a people whose claim to the land relied on force and occupation.

What relationship do Lessing's stories have either with the Rhodesian discourse which is now closed or with any of the multiple discourses which are present at the moment in Zimbabwe? The answers to that question are as necessarily complex as are the stories themselves. I believe that within the stories there is a continual tension between a romantic response to the African bush and the capitalism of the settlers which sought to transform it into profitable settlements, mining or agricultural land. Preben Kaarsholm has argued that the essence of all imperial ideology lies in the contradictory themes of civilisation and nature – a dualism active in bourgeois thinking from Rousseau to Freud. Alongside 'straightforward apologetics of imperialist institutions' and the extolling of 'the progress of capitalist civilization', there is that other discourse of romantic anti-capitalism 'which has as its root a deepfelt unease about the quality of life in the developing centres of the Western world'. For both the promoters of imperialist expansion and consolidation and the romantic anti-capitalist, 'imperialist thinking formulates an alternative to a social system in crisis' (pp. 17–18). If one reads Lessing's stories as explorations of these contradictory themes within imperial discourse, it is possible to see at least one reason why her work should be distanced from the discourses of contemporary Zimbabwe. Capitalism and socialism are the central oppositions in Zimbabwe's discourse and they are conceived within the larger framework of Zimbabwean nationalism. Romantic anti-capitalism is an entirely alien concept, an item in a European discourse, which has not taken root in Zimbabwe. When capitalism is opposed to romanticism, as I believe

it significantly is in Lessing's stories, capitalism assumes a different
character from its character in either socialist or black nationalist
discourse. If one reads Lessing's stories as produced by a European
romanticism rather than as the products of a liberal settler, the
distinction between herself and writers who wrote Africa as
primitive may not be as valid as the *Encyclopedia* entry assumes. A
person becoming spiritually renewed by the epiphanies afforded
by the veld belongs to the same discourse as a man recovering his
manhood in his encounter with the primitive. Lessing's stories, of
course, frequently distance themselves from this discourse. But
my point is that the discourse is not only unacceptable to a
Zimbabwean but depends on a view of the land which would be
unrecognisable to him or her. Nevertheless the opposition was a
real enough opposition in imperial discourse and as such influenced
one way in which the settlers thought of both themselves and
Rhodesia.

White Rhodesians were always torn between their growing sense
of their own nationhood and their awareness of themselves as a
British people confronting wilderness which in Britain had been
tamed many centuries before. Their sense of nationhood led to a
celebration of their economic development of what they chose to
regard as empty land; their sense of themselves as pioneers of the
wilderness allowed them to see themselves as a people more in
touch with nature than those Britons who had stayed at home
could ever be. In most of Lessing's stories there are characters
whose roots lie in Britain or at least in urban South Africa. In all of
the stories veld and town or farmhouse lie in opposition to one
another, syntagms of the Zambesian/Rhodesia–Europe opposition,
which are in turn transformations of the contradictory themes of
nature and civilisation of which Kaarsholm has written. Almost
invariably in Lessing's stories, the narratives reject the towns with
their African townships and suburban sprawl and the space around
the successful farms and mines which has pushed back the
wilderness. If there is inspiration in this country, it lies not in the
towns and farms but in the vastness of the veld beyond them.
Children, who are not yet caught up in the success their parents
pursue, lonely prospectors who will never make a rich strike,
unsuccessful farmers like Dick Turner or Mr Quest are all more
likely to be written as more complexly human because of their
encounter with the veld than the successful farmers and miners
or the settlers in the towns. In the very isolation of those solitary

figures in communion with the veld we can sense the strength of romantic anti-capitalism within Lessing's discourse.

In *Martha Quest* among the eccentric settlers on neighbouring farms is Lord Jamie, who walks naked round his farm, eats only fruit and nuts and quarrels with his wife when she clothes their children for insulting the God who made Adam and Eve (p. 65). In the nature/civilisation paradigm, a sense of the loss of Eden is the mythic expression of the distorted life of the city. Lord Jamie is offered in Martha's narrative with all the force of a mythic character but a more subdued mythopoesis of an attempt to recover Eden can be read again and again in the stories. Sometimes, as in 'A Home for the Highland Cattle', the impulse to Eden is foiled as soon as the immigrant arrives in the colony. The illusion of man living at one with nature is sustained by the appearance of the city – it is 'half-buried in trees' (p. 251)[3] – but it requires money to translate the illusion into a house and garden large enough to harmonise with the vast spaces around the city. In 'Eldorado', a romantic, legendary ancestor, contemptuous of sexual and financial conventions, is invoked by Alec Barnes to justify his contempt for success and the struggle to be better than his neighbours (p. 304). The ancestor's wild glamour, which is fused in the narrative with the reminiscences of a prospector, offers an alternative discourse to the English Alec has rejected as well as to the maternal discourse of Maggie Barnes, which has as its metonymies hard work, solidity, worthwhileness, prosperity and fame. 'Eldorado' incorporates that other denial of Eden, which appears so often in the stories and novels. The settlers may have come to Africa to escape from the commercial grind but many of them soon become caught up in the pursuit of success and, while creating huge and profitable farms, destroy the landscape of vlei and woodland. Alec Barnes's maize lands spread out from the house until they finally reach the farm boundaries and through the ravaged bush revealed the headgear of a gold-mine, a metonymy of the whole complex commercial system from which he had fled in the first place. Only through his mad retreat into gold-divining and his indifference to any profits his discoveries may bring him is he able to retain the romantic discourse which brought him to Africa.

Of the stories which deal with farming, only in '"Leopard" George' does the narrative deny us a view of an agricultural landscape. In fact it insists on the absence of any cultivation in the 'three-mile-long expanse of untouched grass' in front of the house and the contrast between the settled valley and George's own wild acres. Nevertheless George becomes very rich and the narrative emphasises the amount of work he puts into the farm. His labour and his wealth and the virgin veld are thus present as contradictions in the narrative. Entirely absent is the transformed landscape, a transformation which has to take place if he is to become wealthy. In that unexpected silence we are provided with what is, in Lessing's writing, a rare glimpse of the settler idyll: the recoverable Eden but an Eden without primitive inconvenience. In this Eden man lives luxuriously but in harmony with a nature untouched by the hand of man. The fact that the very real luxury achieved by some of the maize farmers in the 1920s was derived from a badly paid black labour force driven from their land by taxation is also apparently evaded for much of the narrative. Labour is a possible problem as George knows when he starts to work the farm but once Old Smoke has come and gathered men about him to work for George, the ordinary recruitment problems on Rhodesian farms of that period vanish. The compound is 'not the usual collection of shambling huts about which no one cared' but 'a proper native village', which men did not leave 'to go "home"' (p. 198). One facet of romantic anti-capitalism, the nostalgia for pre-industrial England, is revealed when the narrative lapses into the sort of nostalgia which is a familiar part of such discourses in the nineteenth century. In the 1920s, 'a more gentle, almost feudal relationship was possible between good masters and their servants: there was space, then, for courtesy, bitterness had not yet crowded out affection' (p. 195). As always in a Lessing narrative, when the narrative voice allows itself the privilege of speaking with the hindsight of actual developments in Rhodesian history, the grasp of history is impeccable. The overcrowding in the reserves became a serious issue only in the 1930s and it took another forty years before the bleak landscape of *Waiting for the Rain* became the landscape of practically all Zimbabwe's Communal Lands. Pressure on the land as much as any other issue politicised the peasants and made them willing allies to the nationalist leadership in the 1950s and 1960s. That development of which Lessing would have been aware when she wrote the story raises the question of whether the settler discourse which wrote the 1920s as a golden age is being ironically subverted at this early point in the narrative. One notes those words 'feudal', 'space', 'courtesy', 'affection' and their opposites 'bitterness' and 'crowded out'. 'Masters and servants' are part of the first set in the early part of the story. They belong to the second set in the historical 1930s, when men and women were forced to migrate to settler farms to look for work. At the end of the story, George's relationship with his labour is like that of any of his neighbours, faced with 'the urgent necessity of attracting new labour' (p. 214). With the 'feudal relationship' between himself and Old Smoke broken and Old Smoke no longer there to provide the authority of the old order, George himself 'would have to provide that focus, with his own will, his own authority; and he knew very well the strain and worry that he would have to face' (p. 214). With Old Smoke's departure George has become like the other settlers in his relationship both to the land and the people of the land, a new conformity which is signalled by his marrying Mrs Whately, the woman whose advances he has repulsed for much of the story.

In his determination to preserve the game on the farm and in his recreation of a traditional native village, George has attempted to keep intact a pre-colonial discourse. The narrative has used the term 'almost feudal' to describe how he has written himself into that discourse and the very anachronism of reading the racial hierarchies of Rhodesia in mediaeval European terms is symptomatic of the European romantic discourse of which for much of the story he is subject. In the destruction of George's idyll the narrative is as it were refusing the very discourse which has apparently produced it. What appeared as perverse silences in the first part of the story can be read not as silences on Lessing's part but silences within romantic anti-capitalist discourse. When we note that the space occupied by the great homestead has no economic relationship with the rest of the farm, we are making present the absence of any rigorous economic awareness within the discourse itself. The wilderness and the house are ideal but discrete statements about Africa on the one hand and the settler in Africa on the other.

When George does invade the other space – the ideal native village – he does so not as someone who is economically active but as the exploiter of a young girl's sexuality. When she in turn invades his space, the separate, racially intact space which the settlers have drawn around their institutions, she has to be punished by exile. It is an exile not to the wilderness to which, in George's discourse, she belongs, but to a mission school. Missions, however much settlers loathed missionaries and their activities, can be read within the nature/civilisation oppositions: as the civilisation of Christianity setting out to quell the heathen nature of Africa. The second girl, whom George sends away when he discovers that she is Old Smoke's wife, is killed by a leopard on her last trip back to the compound. The wilderness is obeying the logic which has been accorded it within the settler discourse, and has taken back the girl who properly belonged to it. Before the girl's death, the veld, the wild animals, the native village are metonymies of a fragile natural order which is both written by and preserved by George. With the girl's death and George's hunt for the leopard, not only is the mutual hostility between settler and wilderness revealed but also the need for such hostility. The seduced wife of a foreman, the dead leopard, whose death arouses no emotion in George, and George's sudden awareness of the bush as frightful presence are metonymies of the settler's encounter with Africa where the brutal, the exploitative and the wary soon become casually necessary attitudes within the whole process of forcing the land to accommodate itself to the capitalist themes within the settler discourse. George may have tried to allow the settler space to co-exist with the space of pre-colonial Africa; and he may have tried to keep intact the two discourses, allowing neither to subvert the other; but at the end of the story, with the game-preservation notices torn down and George recruiting labour like any other settler, the capitalist discourse has replaced that of romantic anti-capitalism and has become as dominant on Four Winds as anywhere else in Rhodesia. The inexplicable absences in the text are revealed as George's futile attempt to be the subject of a discourse which evaded the dominant discourse of Rhodesia and at its end the text refuses the silence which George's discourse has attempted to impose on it.

Usually in the stories, the immigrants, whatever romantic ideas may have motivated them when they arrived, end up by writing themselves into the settler capitalist discourse. Marina's matchmaking with the highland cattle as bait is conducted against the background of her husband's growing conviction of the feckless superstition of the blacks. One of his bush trips is spent 'trying to persuade these blacks' to destock; they have reduced the land to eroded gullies (p. 276); the government should ban lobola (p. 290); it would be a good thing if Theresa miscarried (p. 293). The attitudes behind these remarks belong to the settler discourse which had created reserves as labour supply depots for their own enterprises and then complained how population pressures in the reserves had destroyed the land, the virgin African which the other theme in the discourse celebrated. At the end of the story Marina no longer feels a sense of shock at the routine dehumanisation of Africans. With a house in the suburbs she once despised, searching for an ideal table, she is passed by a file of prisoners, whom, because they are black, she sees but does not really register. Charlie is among them; Theresa following him. In the romantic discourse which has controlled the narrative until this point, the two are given a sharply focused individuality. Now, half-recognising them, she imagines herself mistaken and, using a favourite settler cliché, consigns Charlie to the anonymous black masses: 'he must have reached home by now' (pp. 300–1). Africans always had access to some space beyond that controlled by the settlers which the settlers believed they should call home.

In most of the stories the dominant discourse within which the narrative appears to operate is that of a colonial bourgeoisie. The measurement of success or failure by the success or failure of agricultural or mining enterprises, the attraction and control of labour, the obsession in adults that their children will do well, the creative and sometimes destructive energy with which farms and miners shape the land, all mark the settlers as a bourgeoisie. They may have attempted to escape from the pressures and conformity of bourgeois life abroad but they have simply recreated conditions in which human worth is measured in terms of how far bourgeois aspirations are satisfied or frustrated. Even in a story such as 'Winter in July', where the title signals difference from a European world, the evil which Julia twice glimpses is the evil which derives from living without rules. In this case the rules are those conventions with which the British middle classes arrange their relationships and secure their lives. The 'Winter' and 'July' of the title refer, of course, to Southern Hemisphere seasons but they also refer to the crisis for Julia as she confronts the dead season to which her purposeless life has brought her. The wealth which the brothers have created from their farms allows her not only to live without rules but to be vague about the economic conditions which have made such a life possible. She has managed to exist outside both the romantic anti-capitalist discourse and the capitalist discourse of the successful farmers. The question with which she expresses this crisis; 'What do I contribute to all this?' (p. 240) is directed both to the fields where reaping is in progress and to the sky and earth, dynamic, fecund, purposeful, an energetic system within which the farms must function if they are to prosper. Her own childlessness stands rebuked by the energy around her. It is Kenneth's courtship which precipitates Julia's crisis. He more than Julia's husband has made the farm as prosperous as it is. The fact of his wanting to marry and have children in a story where fecundity and sterility are important textual oppositions writes him within the creative natural order which Julia glimpses. The church wedding and the suitable wife place him within a bourgeois discourse of property, of which heirs and inheritance are metony-mies. In this story, at least, the tropical exuberance the stories so often celebrate is being fused with the creativity of the colonial bourgeoisie. At the end of the story the narrative is being produced from both romantic and capitalist discourses.

Some settler children in the stories seem to refuse their parents' concern with success. They accept the wild space still left on the farms as something which does not require transformation into agricultural land before it can be appropriated to themselves. In 'A Sunrise on the Veld', the exultation which accompanies the movement from farmhouse and the cultivated part of the farm in 'acres of long pale grass' on the vlei (p. 61) echoes an equivalent delight which the young Martha Quest finds in a countryside which her mother reads as threatening. The children may feel at ease with what is to them totally familiar, but invariably their sense of wonder and delight is arrived at as an act of defiance of the adult discourse. As long as he remains in adult space, the boy in 'A Sunrise on the Veld' cannot comprehend the epiphany which the sight of the maimed and dying buck has afforded him: 'Soon the very next morning he would get clear of everybody and go to the bush and think about it' (p. 66). For this child there are spatial constraints on the romantic discourse within which he instinctively writes the wilderness.

In 'The Old Chief Mshlanga', the nostalgia for a rural childhood with which the story begins – 'They were good, the years of ranging the bush over her father's farm' (p. 47) – is quickly rendered more complex than the recollection of a childhood pastoral. The bush does not produce an autonomous identity in the child's imagination but instead its elements are transformed into elements in a European discourse. Mealies and witchweed signify not Africa but stand as signs of a cathedral, a northern witch and the landscape of a northern fairy-story. Only when these European texts have been countered by other texts about the settler occupation of the country does the remark, 'This was the Old Chief's country' (p. 50) signify that the familiar bush cannot so easily be appropriated. It is the subject of an African discourse and arouses as great a nostalgia in its dispossessed people as the narrative subject feels for her childhood when the African bush could so easily be absorbed into a European folk-memory. Both black and white claim the land but, more important, by the end of the story the narrator can no longer innocently make the land serve a European discourse. The adult whites may claim as theirs what once were the Old Chief's lands but the child who has entered Chief Mshlanga's space knows that ownership is read by the blacks as usurpation and destruction. The narrator is no longer a settler confident of herself as subject; she knows she is also a victim. But in this story, as in 'A Sunrise on the Veld', the adult discourse remains unaffected by these sudden surges of insight. With the romantic discourse invalidated by the child's experience, the only way in which the adult discourse can now be opposed is by a radical discourse. Such a discourse would subvert the imperialism which has both created the colony and justifies the settler presence within it. The narrator does not acquire that discourse; instead it is left to the Old Chief himself, speaking through the cook, to formulate the alternative and subversive discourse. As invariably happens in the stories, the white Rhodesian progressive voice, which on occasions could be vociferous, is silent. As the story ends we register it only as an absence.

Within the stories, the bush untouched by towns, settler houses and agriculture becomes the domain of blacks, children and Afrikaners. These metonymies for the space beyond adult, English-speaking settler control can be extended with words such as innocence, savagery, raw, uncultivated. For black Zimbabweans the discourse which can produce such a set is profoundly unattractive. In the primary set they are being written as children as well as being identified with people who in Zimbabwe are seen to have created little except apartheid. In the secondary set they are being written as people who have remained outside the processes of growth and refinement. Nevertheless the presence of Afrikaners in several of the stories reminds us that if they were viewed with dislike by settler capitalism, romantic anti-capitalism in Britain itself saw their peasant independence as an attractive alternative to South Africa's gold and diamond magnates before and during the

Boer War. It is this latter discourse that has produced the Dewets of 'The Dewets Come to Kloof Grange' and the Van Heerdens of 'The Second Hut'.

In the first of these stories, Mrs Gale has created round the farmhouse an English garden of fountains, roses and lawns from which she can look across to a range of hills, ignoring the tropical vegetation along the river and ravine below the house. Mrs Dewet refuses both Mrs Gale's space and the social conventions the space imposes on her, moving instinctively towards the river and revelling sensuously in her heat and scents of a tropical landscape. At the end of the story Mrs Gale has designated both Dewets as savages, a designation made possible in Rhodesian discourse by their being Afrikaners. The ease with which the English-speaking settlers excluded Afrikaners from any fellowship with them is indicated in 'The Second Hut' as soon as Major Carruthers recognises that his new assistant is Afrikaans. Had Van Heerden been of British stock, Carruthers would have found him a place in his house. As an Afrikaner, his quarters are a mud and pole hut standing in uncleared bush. Both the materials of the hut and its surroundings belong to the ubiquitous compounds of the farms rather than to the settler houses, but its isolation from the huts of the workers and from the farmhouse itself suggests how Afrikaners were seen within the British settler discourse to occupy a middle-ground between white and black. In the same way as the Afrikaners in *Children of Violence* refuse this place within the discourse, so both Mrs Dewet and the Van Heerdens make themselves subjects of the wilderness in a way few adult English-speaking settlers do in the stories. The river is 'my river' to Mrs Dewet, a more honest claim to ownership than the 'my mountains' of Mrs Gale (p. 119) since the mountains are separated from her by ravine and river which she dreads. Van Heerden's wife appears to Carruthers as 'the symbol of fecundity, a strong irresistible heave of matter' – images which recall the way in which Lessing so often writes Africa itself. With his children swarming around him, Van Heerden, 'proud . . . of his capacity for making children' (p. 87), has asserted the human both in himself and in the woman who is, in Carruthers's perception, 'force' and 'matter'. He shows a relaxed command of his domestic space which is to Carruthers mere bush. As an Afrikaner he is at ease with Africa, although significantly not with Africans, in a way few of the British settlers in the stories are until they have transformed it into space of which they are clearly the subjects.

I have so far avoided any mention of 'Hunger', the story which it might seem breaks with the discourses and the spaces created by the discourses which, I have suggested, are the important structures of these stories. 'Hunger' is the only story in which a black is the subject of the entire narrative, although in stories such as 'The Old Chief Mshlanga', 'Little Tembi' and ' "Leopard" George' blacks generate important alternatives to the dominant settler discourses. It is from the tension between these black and white discourses that the informing ironies of the narratives derive. But 'Hunger' must stand out from the other stories if only because whites are uniquely absent in it. This, however, raises problems of narrative. How far are whites absent in a story where the black subjects are produced by a white writer? How far is 'Hunger' a product of white ideology even if the ideology is certainly liberal and probably socialist? Such questions, which may seem unacceptably racist in other contexts, assume a very real significance in a country where, as I remarked earlier, blacks are concerned to control the literary discourse of an independent Zimbabwe.

Jabavu in many ways seem to anticipate Lucifer in *Waiting for the Rain*. The two share a scepticism about the values of rural tradition; they both yearn for a place within that space created by the West whether it is simply the settlers' city or in Lucifer's case 'abroad'. There are important differences though. At no stage in *Waiting for the Rain* is Lucifer's discourse unequivocally dominant. The traditional discourse has not lost faith in the very elements which it has created. The constraints of witchcraft and the anger of the ancestors with which it ensures that it shall remain a normative discourse operate as powerfully at the end of the novel as they did at the beginning. Tradition does not have an equivalent authority in 'Hunger'. Instead the subject of the traditional discourse is Jabavu's father, who is helpless to stem the restless migration of young people to mine, farm and city.

'What is happening to our people?' he asked sorrowfully. 'What is happening to our children? Once, in our kraals, there was peace, there was order. Every person knew what it was that they should do and how that thing should be done. The sun rose and sank, the moon changed, the dry season came, then the rains, a man was born and lived and died. We knew, then, what was good and evil.'   (pp. 416–17)

There are elements of negritude in this speech, for negritude asserts as positive values the negative elements in the West's discourse about Africans. The absence of progress in the processes of rural life, which the settlers would have used as evidence of a static barbarism, become to Jabavu's father evidence of the presence of ethical codes producing the security of a public morality. Only a non-African would write Africans as part of the natural order as Lessing has done there. Sun, moon, dry season, rains, man's birth, life and death are metonymies of natural processes but they also deny human creativity and initiative. Muchemwa's rural brother in *The Mourned One* and the traditionalists in *Waiting for the Rain* are written within the traditional discourse as controllers of their natural environment, whether or not other discourses in the novels question the validity of such claims. An alternative view of the past is provided by Jabavu's mother. She recalls tribes from the south terrorising those in the north so that her people spent half their lives 'like rabbits in the kopjes' (p. 417). Zimbabwean readers would recognise in her remarks a recollection of the Ndebele raids on the Shona, which were an important element in colonial historiography and which have now been shown to have been greatly exaggerated both in their frequency and scope. Settler historians justified the occupation precisely because it put an end to Ndebele raiding but it is inconceivable that Zimbabwean historians should justify the invasion of the country on those grounds. In this short exchange between husband and wife, although the fictional subjects of the two discourses are Africans, the sense that they are produced by an author writing within the settler discourse is very strong. Zimbabweans would accept neither account of the past as a valid depiction of pre-colonial Zimbabwe.

These are peripheral elements in the story and deal with issues which would certainly have appeared peripheral in the 1950s to a progressive like Lessing. But in Zimbabwe, where the recovery of an African discourse about the pre-colonial past as well as Rhodesia is seen as morally imperative by cultural nationalism and where there is a widespread belief that colonialism merely interrupted a Zimbabwean historical process, the discourses of Jabavu's father and mother will not be read as peripheral.

The central metaphor of the story is contained in its title. Jabavu's hunger is at first a literal hunger. He was weaned in a year of drought made worse for people by fluctuations in grain prices on the international market and local traders taking advantage of scarcity and raising the price of grain. The second stage of his hunger is a hunger for the things of the settler world: the metonymies of this hunger are soap, a pair of torn shorts, a fragment of mirror, a comb, a hair-parting, a torn comic book and an incomplete alphabet. As the story progresses the set is extended to include brick houses, the uniform of the police and modern methods of crop production. Jabavu's father was content to be objectified by days and season. Jabavu's hunger is a hunger for authority over his own environment. He aspires to write himself as a subject in his world in the same way as he believes the settlers have done. What to the settlers is cast-off rubbish, is to Jabavu a sign both of difference and superiority, both of which are validated in the technological achievements and government hierarchies of the settlers. Once again there is nothing in the narrative to counter its claims that such subject status can be achieved only through the ideology and praxis of the West. In their traditional world Africans remain objectified.

In his pursuit of difference and superiority, Jabavu is pursuing the individual superiority he believes himself to possess and to merit. He has rejected a rural collective identity but he is not willing simply to be absorbed into the collective identities provided by the town: by, on the one hand, the gang of petty thieves; on the other, by membership of the League for the Advancement of the African People. In his fantasies he produces himself as having control of the gang or of being a political leader.

Jabavu has read his difference from the village people as uniqueness and uniqueness as superiority. In showing these transformations in Jabavu, Lessing appears to be writing out of a formula of socialist realism. For the larger narrative counters Jabavu's narrative by insisting on his typicality. He is one of thousands of young men fighting against the constraints of tradition and for a respected place in the town. We see the tension between these two narratives most clearly when he speaks at the League meeting and offers a highly censored narrative of his weeks in town. It is naively produced as the record of a unique experience. It is Mr Samu who designates his experiences as typical, typical of thousands of young men like Jabavu when they come to town (p. 472). In that word 'typical' we read his hunger in a way that

Jabavu is not yet able to read it: the hunger of an entire generation. At the end of the story, after he has been imprisoned, Jabavu's hunger is satisfied. He is awarded the identity he has been unconsciously searching for. Not in individual achievements recognised as exceptional by the settlers but in the 'we' of the black masses of the country, forged into a peasantry and proletariat by settler policies. Jabavu's instinctive revolt against the conditions of his life has at last been channelled into the first stirrings of a revolution against all that settler rule entails.

The end of the story is written within a discourse that was becoming more and more familiar to Zimbabweans in the 1960s and 1970s. Zimbabwe's ruling party is a Marxist–Leninist party and cultural nationalism, if it requires legitimisation, can find it in Lenin's nationalities programme. Many Zimbabwean critics would demand of Zimbabwean fiction that it shows Engels' typical characters in typical situations. Nevertheless it is possible to read the story as a more orthodox Marxist narrative than any we have so far seen in this country. Without the modern political organisation provided by the League, which is in turn a creation of settler society, Jabavu is simply the Big Mouth. He is at once the boastful youth, hopelessly unaware of the world in which he is making his way as well as the child greedy for a sustenance he has as yet done nothing to deserve. It is Marxist orthodoxy that a politicised proletariat emerges dialectically from the capitalism which made its existence as a proletariat possible. Only eight years after independence it is perhaps difficult in Zimbabwe not to see the colonial era as an irrelevant but brutal intervention in Zimbabwe's history. It is certainly hard to see it as an agency of progress, a necessary, if unlovely, stage without which neither peasantry nor proletariat would have come into being. Jabavu yearning for the consumer products of the West and Jabavu politicised into part of a modern revolutionary consciousness are productions of the dialectical process colonialism set in motion. It is the pre-colonial past not colonialism which the story writes as irrelevant.

What I have suggested in this chapter is that Lessing's stories stand apart from the dominant discourses of Zimbabwe, whether those are cultural nationalist or a Marxist discourse inscribed by cultural nationalism. The *Encyclopedia Zimbabwe* article appeared to marginalise Lessing because she was white and because the sense of a Zimbabwean nation is not sufficiently strong in her work.

Considering the period when she lived in this country, no one should find this lack of awareness surprising, for even in the early 1950s the collapse of European empires in Africa was impossible to foresee. The fact that the empires did collapse and in the 1960s and 1970s the African nations we know today were created had a profound effect on literary discourses in Zimbabwe. Our independence came late but when it did come there were flourishing literatures in English, French and Portuguese from all parts of the continent. Even before independence Zimbabweans had written themselves as subjects of a literature in English, as we have seen. At independence, African literatures not only provided models for our literature which made the metropolitan models redundant but also produced texts in which Africans wrote themselves as subjects of African discourses. The propositions and counter-propositions of an African debate was defined and were being argued. It was with some relief that Zimbabweans could take part in such a debate and forget the settler ideologies which had absorbed so much of their attention for so many years. Cultural nationalism could now be both Zimbabwean and at times pan-Africanist. But we still have to confront the fact that cultural nationalism, however wide or narrow its base, is still only an ideology of Zimbabwean history. If it fails to recognise that Zimbabwe's base is Rhodesia, it is guilty of silence about a central fact of our history. Lessing's oppositions of settler capitalism and romantic anti-capitalism may no longer be relevant items in a Zimbabwean discourse. The emergence of African bureaucracies and African bourgeoisies and their relationship with the peasant masses are, however, central concerns of much African literature. The debate between town and country, between capitalist and peasant modes of production still continues. Peasants and veld may be written differently in Zimbabwe to the way in which Lessing wrote them, but her art recognises equivalent tensions to those which are familiar today and her discourse around those tensions refuses closure.

Notes

1. Wilbur Smith, Daniel Carney and Michael Hartmann (who is referred to as John).
2. The Reserves were called Tribal Trust Lands in the 1960s and 1970s. They are now known as Communal Lands.
3. All page references to Lessing's stories are from *African Stories*.

Works Cited

Kaarsholm, Preban. 'Imperialism, Ideology, Romantic Anti-Capitalism and J. A. Hobson' in 'Imperialism and Romantic Anti-Capitalism: Four Papers on Culture and Ideology c. 1890'. *Kultur og Samfund* I. Institute VI, Roskilde Universitets-center, 1983. pp. 17–25.

Kahari, George P. *Aspects of the Shona Novel and Other Related Genres.* Gweru: Mambo Press, 1986.

Lessing, Doris. *African Stories.* New York: Touchstone Press, 1981.

——,*Martha Quest.* London: Michael Joseph, 1952.

Muchemwa, Kizito, ed. *Zimbabwean Poetry in English.* Gwelo: Mambo Press, 1978.

Mungoshi, Charles L. *Waiting for the Rain.* London: Heinemann, 1975.

Samkange, Stanlake. *On Trial for My Country.* London: Heinemann, 1966.

——, *The Mourned One.* London: Heinemann, 1975.

——, *Year of the Uprising.* London: Heinemann, 1978.

Tabex Encyclopedia Zimbabwe, ed. Katherine Sayce *et al.* Harare: Quest Publishing, 1987.

2

The Quest and the Quotidian: Doris Lessing in South Africa

EVE BERTELSEN

INTRODUCTION

Doris Lessing's *Bildung*, or life-search, as formulated in her fictional texts is read by Lessing critics as the symbolic history of the age. This is not unprecedented. Such 'reflectionism' is a central fallacy of our literary history. For example, D. H. Lawrence's proposal that the Industrial Revolution began in the Eastwood of his boyhood and was finally exorcised in the woods of the Chatterley estate is a received fact of literary education. The motivation for such cultural fallacies is buried deep in the *Zeitgeist* and cannot be addressed here. What I aim to investigate on a more modest scale is one local pattern of reception of Lessing's *oeuvre* that calls into question generalisations regarding the 'universal' significance and quality of her work. The South African reception of Lessing is instructive, not because of the quality of local reviews (they are unsophisticated on the whole), but because that small white elite from which both readers and critics are drawn is the author's point of origin. Whereas these texts are, elsewhere, read bifocally – both as an ongoing pilgrim's progress and as documents of unquestioned historical veracity, they strike the South African reader as raw and highly problematical representations of the quotidian – the riven beauty, grotesquerie and injustice which is our daily life.

The early Lessing, her texts and her local reviewers are the product of a shared set of cultural relations: the political/cultural matrix that may be designated colonial Rhodesia and apartheid South Africa. Appendix A correlates major events in Southern Africa from the 1950s to the 1980s with the publication of Lessing's texts, and offers a brief characterisation of each decade's reviews.

41

For all of its sins of reduction, such a schema is illuminating: it offers at least *one* explanation for the dramatic rise, and equally dramatic fall of Lessing's reputation in the subcontinent, a pattern that seems to be the opposite of that of Europe and the United States. It may be felt that this over-politicises the work. My answer would be that *everything* in South Africa is political, and the reception of Lessing particularly so. The text which the South African reads is *not the same text* that is appropriated by the foreign reader: in Haus Jauss's terms the reader 'completes the text' differently, operating within the different social codes of knowledge and a historically specific frame of reference.

For a start, Lessing is well known to most of these reviewers as a historical person. During the 1950s and 1960s her activities were well documented in the local press; in media language she became an 'elite person' or 'media known', a troublesome and famous local girl. Her political pronouncements, her divorce and departure for England, the publication of her early books, were all items of common conversation. There is scarcely a member of the older intelligentsia who does not claim to have known her personally or possess anecdotes about her public and private life. Given this plethora of information it is difficult to isolate precisely those factors which have determined her local reputation. The reviewers, invariably English, white and middle class, produce a series of finite, historical readings which are an amalgam of biographical data, common-sense assumptions about a 'good read', political prejudices and attempts at objective analysis of the texts *qua* texts. On the whole the books are read as expressive realist documents or thinly fictionalised autobiography. A notable feature of most reviews is that the critics appear to have *all* of Lessing's books, and take pains to supply cross-references. The reviewers all applaud her 'promise' and eagerly anticipate from her pen that chimera, the 'Great South African Novel', which, as the decades unroll, it becomes abundantly clear that she is not likely to deliver!

In the body of this paper I adopt the three-part schema suggested by my outline. I periodise the problem into decades, offering first a brief historical sketch which I then correlate with Lessing's publications and their critical reception. In this way I hope to show a marked (indeed, antithetical) divergence in the developing imperatives of South African life and Lessing's personal and artistic concerns. The movement is aptly summed up in my title: as Lessing focuses on *inner space* (and its allegorical projection into cosmic parable), the Southern African contest over *public space/social space* escalates on a sliding scale, to the point where the author's present disparagement of group initiatives *per se* runs directly counter to the felt effect of our experience.

THE FIFTIES

The Afrikaner Nationalist Government of South Africa, which is still in office, comes to power in 1948 and begins to implement its policy of apartheid – a coercive rewriting of the informal racism of colonial times. The 1950s see an important realignment of both black and white politics which will affect the daily life of both groups for the decades to come. In 1950 the Communist Party of South Africa (SACP) is banned, and resistance politics is subsequently organised under the banners of the Pan Africanist Congress (PAC) and the African National Congress (ANC). A Defiance Campaign is initiated against the compulsory carrying of 'passes' by blacks. This begins a mass mobilisation of blacks which will culminate in the Sharpeville Massacre of March 1960. In Rhodesia, the 'Federation' of what are now Zimbabwe, Zambia and Malawi attempts to consolidate white rule in the territory to the north, by pooling resources and offering a paternalistic 'partnership' to blacks.

It is into this reality that Lessing's earliest texts are written. her Rhodesian experiences of the 1940s engage all of the important elements of the period: racism; the threat to white ascendancy posed by both socialism and African nationalism, and the personal dilemma of whites as they attempt to align their European values and sensibilities with both the stark reality of the land itself and new threats to their controlling interests. To the South African reviewer Lessing's fictional representations are thus urgent, compelling and of personal concern.

The Grass Is Singing (1950)

Lessing's first novel anticipates most of her later concerns and provides a microcosm of her future styles. In an apparently simple tale of an unhappy marriage narrated in a romantic mode, she explores issues of the individual versus the collective, colonial mores, sanity and madness and the potential destructiveness of both family and male–female relationships. Contemporaneous reviews of GS[1] share a common pattern: all commend Lessing's art and writing skill while taking issue with her treatment of local problems. There is a notable parasitism on the London reviews, which are usually quoted and are summarised in detail in accompanying news articles. What seems to be common cause is that while Lessing imaginatively penetrates the landscape and its people, her art is vitiated by her intrusion of political opinions coupled with an unacceptable stereotyping of colonial characters. Strong dislike for the author's 'piety', even 'misanthropy', is present in most reviews. W.J.P.B. in the *Rand Daily Mail* (11 March 1950) under the heading 'Writer's Grim Story of an African Farm' details Lessing's Rhodesian career, and quotes UK reviews which 'rightly praise' the book. However, he finds the claim that the novel offers 'a merciless study of South Africa herself' an 'unnecessary and nonsensical exaggeration'. None of the characters, he claims, is *the* local farmer, servant, etc. Although the story is more than 'just another clever South African novel with a bias' and abounds in 'acute observation, accuracy and imagination', 'real and complete in the artistic sense' it cannot possibly be '*all* South Africa'. Anon. in the *Star* (26 March 1950) insists that s/he actually read the novel for a local publisher who turned it down, hence the heading 'Novel that was Rejected in S.A.'. It deserves 'all the encomiums showered on it by English reviewers'. The shower is augmented here with phrases such as 'passion, insight . . . power and sweep that command admiration and awe'. The 'rare realism' of depictions of the farm, labourers, natural settings and 'conjugal scenes of frayed nerves' is noted. But (there is always a 'but') there is a major flaw: even though the 'sordid aspect' is mitigated by her 'perfection of phrase' for the most part, she loses her detachment in places and intrudes her views on 'South Africa's indigenous problems, poor-whiteism and the colour bar'. An intriguing footnote informs us that the novel's original title was *Black and White*, which suggests that the final title and epigraph were added after Lessing's arrival in London. A second review in the *Star* (anon., 17 April 1950) is entitled 'White Defeat in Africa: Gifted Young Woman's Bitter Novel about Rhodesia'. The commentary here pulls together the misgivings of earlier reviewers in an explicit attack on Lessing's 'morbid story of horrible defeat'. It recognises the cruel cycle of Mary's 'poor white' existence, the doomed projects of the ineffectual Dick, and the unspoken prejudices of the settlers, all of which are accurately drawn. What it finds intolerable is the overall tone, characterised as one of 'bitter strength, but almost no humour': the book *could* be 'a South African *Bovary* – but unlike Flaubert, Lessing has not produced a pure work of art; it is mainly meant to convey social judgements'. Anthony Delius, doyen of South African reviewers, takes up all of these points in a more measured piece in the critical journal *Standpunte* (5 March 1951). Under a title 'Study in Black and White' he bemoans the tyranny exercised upon the South African novel by 'The Problem/The Colour Question'. He deplores the exploitation of this issue by what he calls 'cash-crop' authors who cash in on the enduring worldwide interest in local problems. His discussion of *GS* centres again on the two aspects of efficient writing and unacceptable standardisation of character and ideas. He finds it, for all its artistry, 'a very dreary story indeed'. There is only one character Lessing does not dislike and find actively distasteful, and that is Dick (shades of her real father?). As for Mary, so much drabness is unrelentingly heaped upon her, she is 'so inanimate, so insupportably dull and febrilely bitter' as to become a symbol of failure rather than a human being: 'The book is rigged as a "romance-in-reverse" from p. 1 to p. 256 and permeated with dislike . . . serving those with a literary interest in colour problems.' He dissects the plot in some detail, finding the ending 'improbable and unconvincing'; after much contrivance, a desperate 'filling in of gaps' only explicable in terms of myths of the 'voodoo haunted wastes of Africa'. But it is the stereotyping of character which he most dislikes: 'Sex-starved woman, futile husband, "great buck nigger", colonials who stick together, nebulous public school Englishman – this is not Rhodesian society, but a familiar fictional world. Even the whipping is a parody – Simon Legree stuff.' He concludes that Lessing has fallen into the trap of standardising human beings to serve abstract ideas and social problems, leaving the central dilemma of South African writing unsolved: 'how to combine man with his sociological problems without being dwarfed by abstractions in the process'.

For the purposes of this short study the reviews of *GS* serve as a paradigm case. In spite of the author's acknowledged writing skill, reviewers uniformly reject what they read as her misanthropy and pessimism *vis-à-vis* the local scene.

This Was the Old Chief's Country (1951)

Lessing's first short stories appear less contentious to reviewers
than *GS*. The consensus is that they are finely worked and offer a
multifaceted and penetrating picture of Rhodesian life. Anon. in
the *Star* (12 April 1951) sees them 'taking the mask off Africa'.
Lessing gives the 'mystery' of Africa as a set of 'genuine social
tensions exposed on the nerves': husband–wife, farmer–tenant,
employer–servant are all duly recognised, and the accuracy of
Lessing's portrayals is applauded. Particular note is made of her
ability to 'uncover the hinterland of emotion which drives people
to crises quite unrelated to the immediate cause of upset'. M.M.W.
in the *Sunday Times* notes that most of the stories were written
before *GS* (these readers have, of course, read many of them in
local journals in the late 1940s), and that they form the basis for
the themes and layout of the novel. She is the first reviewer to
remark on Lessing's 'recurring characters and themes', for example,
her 'disgruntled settle views' and 'delicate arresting landscapes'.
Though she finds the collection uneven, she selects 'The Nuisance'
and 'Winter in July' as the best, and repeats the split verdict which
is to become commonplace: 'uncommon creative vigour and bitter
perceptiveness'.

Retreat to Innocence (1956) and *Going Home* (1957)

In marked contrast to the distribution of overseas attention, in
South Africa these two books were received more seriously than
the more 'mature' texts and created heated debate. Again, this
is best explained in relation to political developments in the
subcontinent. Lessing's reputation as a 'communist' far outran her
literary fame, and the strenuous clampdown on leftist activities
was probably the running story of the decade.

   RI appeared shortly after several major news stories about
Lessing's return to Rhodesia to write *GH* under contract to the
Soviety news agency, Tass, and her expulsion from South Africa
at Jan Smuts Airport. 'Rhodesian authoress not allowed to enter
S.A. tells of her Political and Racial Dilemmas' gives the 'news
angle' to the first review in the *Sunday Times* (Anon., 15 April
1956).

   In an avuncular overview we are told of Lessing's 'considerable
literary gift', her 'pro-Native sympathies' and her 'impatience with

colonial snobbery'. She is an author with 'a political bias and a sense of mission'. *RI*, although not 'negrophile' comes, then, as no surprise. The tension between Brod (Polish Jew, communist, agitator and idealist) and Julia Barr (midnight wanderer, torn between her impatience with English good taste and her impatience with revolution) is read as straight autobiography. The prodigal local daughter, now in London, is, like Brod, 'taking a breather before the next step'; this is clearly 'a halt in her literary and political journey'. Although as art it is 'disappointing', as an index of Lessing's political dilemma it is of consuming interest to people 'back home'.

On 14 May 1956 the *Star* said: 'Doris Lessing Deserts the Veld for London'. There is a certain relish in reviewers' accounts of the author's continuing battles (now that distance allows of more detached assessment). Here Brod's 'didacticism' and Julia's 'egoism and simplicity', which produce 'a love affair via quarrels', are read again as Lessing's own internal *impasse* which remains unresolved. *GH* gets shorter shrift. It is a direct intervention in politics, and, reviewers make clear, an unacceptable one. The *Rhodesia Herald* (2 May 1957) says it all: 'Communist Doris Lessing Writes Book Attacking Federation'. This is less a review than a *pot pourri* of biography, gossip and speculation: she has no credentials as a journalist; she was allowed in only 'by accident', she misquotes interviewees, etc. It concludes: 'Is Doris Lessing still a communist? There are rumours that she resigned from the Party over Hungary, but at the recent Conference of the Communist Party in London a delegate praised Lessing as their "novelist in the Party".'

Oliver Walker in the *Star* (26 June 1957) also begins by recalling news items. The title announces 'Novelist Given a Tarred White Feather in Bulawayo'. She was tailed throughout her visit; accused of 'putting ideas into the munts' heads' ('munt': an offensive mode of reference to an African). Walker quotes the Africans' preference for apartheid over 'British hypocrisy' in Rhodesia and stresses Lessing's point that, anomalously, the chief support for abolishing the industrial colour-bar at that time comes from white industrialists rather than black labour.

Children of Violence: Martha Quest (1953); *A Proper Marriage* (1954); *A Ripple from the Storm* (1958)

The early Martha Quest novels mark the peak of Lessing's South African fame. With the arrival of each book news items put on display rave notices from the likes of C. P. Snow and Margharita Laski ('best in the English-speaking world', 'moving and flawless', etc.). While local reviewers would like to welcome a major talent, they still detect much unworked autobiographical material, and find the novels turgid, clichéd and schematic.

Of *MQ* Anon. in the *Star* (22 January 1953) writes: 'the lonely farm, a dismal failure to come to grips with the African veld – the standard elements we have grown accustomed to expect. Miss Lessing has done this sort of thing before.' Delius (*Standpunte* 7.3 April 1953) finds her didacticism unchanged: 'Miss Lessing will now reveal to you the the secrets and spiritual horrors of life in the colonies.' The parents are 'casebook characters, contemptuously described'; political discussions are 'clumsy and incredible . . . a crude attempt at sketching in of "background"'; Martha's intellectual activity is 'merely *ascribed* to her', and even nature is 'a mere afterthought in the context'. In place of Snow's 'daemon' Delius finds 'spatters of intellectual irritation' and a 'drab realism' in which spiritual and erotic progress are 'alas, a little standardised'. There are redeeming features: Binkie's character is original and full, and the Club scenes are 'superb'. 'Martha's passivity and somnambulism are neither dark nor deep enough, and merely serve to atrophy the narrative'.

PM and *RFS* get similar treatment. Their style is, in turns, 'starkly photographic' and 'woefully turgid'. Jack Cope in the *Cape Times* (November 1954) deplores the caricatures of 'conceited and stupid administrators and female rulers with their fatuous conventions'. But most of all it is the narrowness of vision he condemns: 'Around the whites are shapes, sounds and echoes of the dark millions. Yet they never intrude for a minute into the self-contained life from eye-opener to sundowner and beyond. Lessing's camera shutter clicks: all the group are there, but outside the circle of the lens is something else, a larger reality that would completely change the perspective were the view to be widened.' This is not the same complaint as Anon.'s (*Star* 11 November 1954) about 'long passages on Martha's post-natal and obstetrical problems that could be easily gleaned from any handbook on motherhood', but it registers a similar frustration with a clinical and restricted text. Cope is no kinder to *RFS* (*Argus* 10 December 1958), where he finds Lessing's autobiography and 'painful self-analysis' full of searing contempt for white colonials as well as 'guilt and self-loathing': 'Over 200 weary pages Martha uses the Communists to reject her own class.' The novel is a cruel caricature of what it might have been: it lacks technical control – she must learn to 'eliminate surplusage'.

It would appear that in the period of Lessing's major 'African' output, while she is being fêted in London as an exciting addition to the literary scene, on her home ground, although she is widely read, critics are more harsh. They reject what they see as her misanthropy and pessimism about the local scene, and find her work promising but artistically flawed.

THE SIXTIES

The sixties begin with Sharpeville and the banning of both the PAC and ANC, whose leaders are committed to prison for life. In Rhodesia Smith tries to 'go it alone' and stave off black majority rule by a unilateral declaration of independence (UDI). Resistance politics in Southern Africa move underground, with the Sabotage Campaign in SA and the beginnings of the Bush War in Rhodesia.

In this period Lessing reworks her political experience of the 1940s in *GN* and the last two novels of *Children of Violence*, *LL* and *FGC*. South African reviewers are unsympathetic both to what they see as 'outdated' material and the author's refocusing of her critical eye on British resistance politics and intellectual fashions.

The Golden Notebook (1964)

Where more dispassionate readers find a major 'epistemological break' in *GN*, to the locals the novel is on a clear continuum with her previous productions. Reviewers find in it the same elements, the same reductive view of the world; it is the 'Doris' we all know making another 'self-conscious attempt at originality'! The title of the *Star* review (24 May 1962) is typical: 'Doris Lessing Appears in Wulf's Clothing.' Lessing's claim that here she 'attempts to break . . . certain forms of consciousness and go beyond them' leaves local reviewers untouched. On the whole they list the contents of the four notebooks in terms of themes and plot: the veld; love affairs; mental illness; the Party – the general feeling being that 'Mrs Lessing has done this all before, but more coherently'. There are fewer reviews now. Anon. in the *Star* reduces the book to its 'standard elements', identifies Anna's 'bestselling novel' as *The Grass Is Singing* and goes on to read the novel as autobiography. 'The love scenes are described with a complete lack of restraint . . . As a realist-recorder with a liking for clinical details . . . Anna lags only a little way behind the author of *Ulysses'*(!) It is 'an amorphous book, admirable in many of its parts, but unsatisfactory as a whole. What ground, technically or in relation to the "frontiers of consciousness" has been broken? None at all, if the truth be told . . . It is merely another testament of disillusion – spiritual, political and sexual.'

Nancy Baines in the *Cape Times* (27 June 1962) sees little more to recommend it. Although she pays more attention to the author's stated intentions, she feels that Lessing has 'missed opportunities': she doesn't exploit different styles of writing; much of it is 'just second-rate'; its repetitions are unjustified, as they don't serve to reveal different sides of Anna's personality. She feels that Anna writes Lessing's own epitaph: 'Yet I am incapable of writing the only kind of novel which interests me: a book powered with an intellectual or moral passion strong enough to create order, to create a new way of looking at life.' South African reviewers' hopes that Lessing might be the author who will produce just such a book for South Africa move into sharp decline at this point, never really to be revived.

Landlocked (1965) and *The Four-Gated City* (1969)

The last two volumes of *Children of Violence* are greeted with disappointment. Lewis Nkosi, Lessing's only local black reviewer, compares Lessing with Nadine Gordimer under the heading 'Les Grandes Dames'. They are both 'wickedly intelligent, and know enough of the jungle to sheath their knives in their garters'. But in spite of spirited 'flashes of steel', Lessing's prose is that of a recorder, 'pedestrian, workaway, adequate, rarely rising to . . . lyricism'. While he admires Martha's 'unflinching' quest which alienates her from family, child, friends and Party, he asserts that Lessing, is, through it all, too close to Martha: 'She is the figure through which moral judgement is passed on all the others. *But who judges her?* It is hardly explained how she avoids the lies in wartime Zambesia where *everyone* lived by lies and dissimulation. *Is she human enough?* (my italics). This review in *New African* (4 September 1965) aptly summarises the misgivings of the majority of the reviewers I have been discussing above: Lessing's realism coupled with what is seen to be an overbearing political and moral piety are uniformly disliked. When *FGC* arrives on the local scene, Lessing's promise evaporates. There is general agreement that something has gone irredeemably wrong with both her literary plans and her judgement. (What this of course means is that there is no longer any hope that she will indeed write the Great South African Novel which the critics had planned for her.) M.M.W. in the *Sunday Times* (1 June 1969) finds the 'usual competent writing, but without purpose'. After a 'long and rather dreary recital' of Martha's further disillusionment (now with London, its people and all its worthy causes) 'at a loss what to do with her characters, she wafts them into the future . . . pursuing desperate causes with mutated children'. She concurs with the *Rand Daily Mail* reviewer (5 September 1969) that 'as the conclusion of an initially sober saga about Martha and her generation, this all seems too sudden'.

The reviews of the sixties persist in reading Lessing's new experimental texts as autobiographical and realist. They see a direct continuity with the obsessional themes of the earlier books, as well as their artistic patchiness and lack of sympathy and warmth. They tend to regard the evolution of her new mystical personae as the logical extension of a Martha (it is implied, a Doris Lessing) who was, anyway, never quite human: always disdainful of her peers, who 'used' people, context and experience to sharpen (as Nkosi puts it) the knife of her wit.

THE SEVENTIES

The rallying call of the seventies is 'solidarity' and the mobilisation of group pressures against the apartheid state. Amidst strikes, boycotts and marches on all fronts, the ANC entrenches its leadership in resistance politics, and the new Botha government embarks on its series of neo-apartheid reforms. At the end of this decade the Bush War forces free elections in Zimbabwe and there is a resurgence of mass struggle in South Africa. Socialist ideas achieve wide popularity amongst blacks in both countries.

My point with regard to Lessing's work of the seventies is very simple: the revolution that she abandoned in 1950 as a lost cause has finally hit the subcontinent. In the midst of social and political turmoil Lessing's contempt for politics and her exclusive concentration on individual interiority strikes the Southern African reader as nothing short of bizarre.

Briefing for a Descent into Hell (1971); Summer Before the Dark (1973); Collected African Stories (1973); Memoirs of a Survivor (1974)

Of the books of the 1970s only *BDH* and the reprinted *AS* are deemed to merit reviews. Even then, the reviewers try to link *DH* with *Children of Violence*, and after a few dismissive comments, prefer to see it as another aberration: 'the least distinguished of her long list of novels' (*Sunday Times*, 2 May 1971) or 'I trust this is a theme she wanted to get off her chest and that she will now ascend from hell to the path she has trodden so successfully in the past' (*Rand Daily Mail*, 2 July 1971). (After all this frustration reviewers fall with glee upon the reprints of *AS* in 1973. I have listed these reviews, but do not intend to discuss them here, since they more or less repeat the accolades of 1951.) If there are any reviews of *SBD* or *MS* I have not been able to trace them.

Reviews of Lessing's work appear to dry up in the 1970s, although her achievements as a 'famous daughter' are still newsworthy. In spite of attempts to make connections between these new works and the earlier African texts, reviewers seem to resign themselves to the fact that Lessing has very little of interest to say after the 1960s to South African readers.

THE EIGHTIES

In 1980 Robert Mugabe wins a landslide victory and Zimbabwe is declared independent. At the same time the ANC resolves on a campaign of urban insurgency in South Africa, aimed to 'make the country ungovernable'. Massive school boycotts, strikes and grassroots community resistance campaigns achieve great success. The government responds by implementing its 'new constitution' with separate chambers in parliament for Coloured and Indians, and declaring a series of nationwide states of emergency under which tens of thousands are detained and many hundreds killed by police and troops.

This is the period of *Canopus*, *Somers* and *GT*, which continue to expose human error on two fronts, the transhistorical/cosmic and the minutely localised. Lessing's final rejection of group endeavour and her (belated) commendation of 'unremembered acts of kindness and of love' could not possibly run more counter to the South African experience if she had expressly planned it that way. In *Canopus*, for example, her epic ambitions give rise to a portmanteau form in which earlier themes and styles are rehearsed and recast: realist, didactic or allegorising narrators in turn pursue issue of male and female energies, technology versus nature, the tyranny of ideologies, and above all, an obsessive search for mind-space and the free life of the imagination.

Canopus (1979–82); *The Diaries of Jane Somers* (1984); *The Good Terrorist* (1985); *The Fifth Child* (1988)

Tony Morphet in the *Sunday Times* (18 August 1980), reviewing *Sirian Experiments*, aptly brings this review of reviews to a close. The heading is (still!) 'Doris Lessing Sticks to the Same Old Theme': 'Social fact, the injustice of life in society and "the group mind" as the condition of evil is her obsession still. Intricate, ambiguous truths have never held much interest for her.' He sees her casting her 'millennial vision' now, over good and evil, 'the long, bloody sequence of injustice that is the earth's history'. He comments on 'the unconvincing though relentless resolution with which she pursues her case', and 'the dreadful, thudding dullness of her prose which leaves me weary and unsatisfied. . . . The novel gives us not the evil of the world, but the enduring obsessions of the author.'

Somers, *The Good Terrorist* and *The Fifth Child* are not taken up by reviewers at all, apart from the odd news item on Lessing's literary 'hoax' and her continuing interest in 'madness' and 'evil'. One would have thought that a novel about urban terrorism, at least, would be of interest to readers who are searched for explosives on daily trips to the supermarket. It seems, though, that the later Lessing's dismissive treatment of this very real issue offers nothing of interest to the South African reader of the 1980s. The few comments on the last two volumes that I have heard are totally dismissive, the feeling being that Lessing's presumption has this time gone too far. Terrorism is yet another 'cash-crop' theme. And how can an author who has spent the past three decades of her life assiduously removing herself from political debate and the arena of activist politics possibly be expected to say anything illuminating about them?

A parallel development, and one that Lessing particularly detests, is that she has latterly been taken up as something of a 'museum piece' by South African academics, chiefly on the basis of her early 'colonial' fiction, now the subject of several scholarly articles, theses and critical books.

CONCLUSION

I began by asserting that the text which the South African reads is not the same text as that read by an American or European. I have offered an account of Lessing's reception in the subcontinent which stresses the specific social knowledge and historical circumstances which produce this body of reviews. The immediacy of Lessing herself and the historical experience which she shares with these reviewers appears to rank highly among these determinants. Her contemporaries on the liberal English press are all critical of apartheid and several are acknowledged 'leftists'. Very few reviewers take issue with her anti-racism or her criticism of colonial mores; it is her contemptuous tone that they reject, and an art which they read, against the evidence of their own senses, as reductive and pessimistic. My second argument is more speculative. In correlating major shifts in South African politics and social life with what I see as an antithetical development in Lessing's discourse, I try to account for a marked decline of interest in her work. In a society where the most intimate of human affairs are still oppressively controlled by legislation it is not possible to entertain a contempt for group solidarity and politics. Indeed, such a position seems scarcely 'human' at all.

Note

1. Throughout this chapter Lessing's works have been abbreviated as follows: *AS/CAS: Collected African Stories; BDH: Briefing for a Descent into Hell; FC: The Fifth Child; FGC: The Four-Gated City; GH: Going Home; GN: The Golden Notebook; GS: The Grass Is Singing; GT: The Good Terrorist; HL: The Habit of Loving; LL: Landlocked; MD: Mr Dolinger; MQ: Martha Quest; MS: Memoirs of a Survivor; NMM: The Story of a Non-Marrying Man and Other Stories; OCC: This Was the Old Chief's Country; PM: A Proper Marriage; PWT: Play with a Tiger; RFS: A Ripple from the Storm; RI: Retreat to*

Innocence; *SBD*: *The Summer Before the Dark*; *SE*: *The Sirian Experiments*;
Somers: *The Diary of Jane Somers*; *TBN*: *The Truth about Billy Newton*.

Work Cited

Jauss, Hans Robert. *Towards an Aesthetic of Reception*, tr. Timothy Bahti.
   Minneapolis: University of Minnesota Press, 1982. Especially pp. 46–75.

Appendix A

DORIS LESSING AND SOUTH AFRICA

1950s

History

1948	Afrikaner Nationalist Government (1948–).
1950	Communist Party of SA banned.
	Defiance Campaign (against passes etc., whole decade).
1956	Treason trial of leaders of Congress Alliance – all acquitted.
1959	PAC, Progressive Party formed.

Summary: Realignment of black/white politics; mass mobilisation of blacks
begins; [Rhodesia: Federation experiment].

Texts

GS (1950); *OCC* (1951); *MQ* (1953); *PM* (1954); *RI* (1956); *GH* (1957); *RFS*
(1958).

Lessing works through politics of 1940s/1950s in SA. Rejects both colonial
values and socialism. Dual concern = social system and its
determinations + personal evolution. Writes out of and into central SA
dilemmas: race; nationalism vs socialism; redundancy of white liberal
politics; dilemmas of individual.

Reviews

Reviewers identify with Lessing's projects. Read texts as autobiographical,
documentation. Commend her writing skill. Recognise accuracy of depiction of local issues and 'types', but deplore schematic features and
'bitterness'/'piety' of author/persona.

1960s

History

1960	Urban defiance against pass laws.
	Sharpeville: demonstrators killed.
	ANC, PAC banned.
1961	Republic of SA declared.
	SA leaves the Commonwealth.
1964	Rivonia treason trial: Mandela, Mbeki and others get life senten-
	ces.
1965	Smith declares UDI in Rhodedsia, backed by SA Government.
1966	Verwoerd stabbed by white extremist.
	Implementation of apartheid proceeds.

Summary: Group areas proclaimed – removal of blacks to 'homelands' (1960s–1970s); crackdown on black organisations; Black mass mobilisation underground; sabotage campaign; Focus 1960–1980s on extra-parliamentary politics; [Rhodesia: UDI and 'Bush War'].

Texts

GN (1962); *LL* (1965); *FGC* (1969).

Reworks politics of 1950s retrospectively. Becomes mediated as symbolic discourse, as she selects to concentrate on personal integrity of expatriate persona, especially as member of highly evolved elite (ESP etc.). Now exposes 'British' panaceas (protest politics, psychiatry, CND).

Reviews

Persist in reading texts as biographical, realist. Remark on repetitive reworking of outdated local material and stereotyping. Unsympathetic towards fragmented and exploratory techniques. See evolution of 'mystical' personae as logical extension of earlier rejections.

1970s

History

1970s	Black trade unions established.
	SA supports insurgents in Angola.
	Mozambique ('border war').
	Continued support for Smith.

1976+   School pupils mobilise. Killed by police at Soweto.
        Continuing strikes, boycotts, marches.
1979   Botha replaces Vorster as head of Nationalist Government.
        Neo-apartheid reforms and 'separate chambers' constitution
        mooted.

Summary: ANC ascendancy in black politics; polarisation of pro-socialist (black) and pro-capitalist (white) politics; white 'reform' programmes begin; resurgence of mass struggle nationwide; [Rhodesia: 'Bush War' forces free elections].

Texts

BFG (1971); *NMM* (1972); *Cas* and *SBD* (1973); *MS* (1974); *Canopus* (1979–82).

Concentrates exclusively on 'inner space' of psyche to exclusion of politics. Social pressures signified as hostile to individual integrity.
    In *Canopus*, again reworks her political history as 'meta-discource' of world and galactic history. Seeks to expose totality of human error on cosmic scale.

Reviews

Decline in interest in texts, although Lessing is newsworthy as 'famous daughter'. Read 'same old obsessions' (rejection of groups; piety; didacticism, etc.) into new 'intimist' texts. Imply that she has little to say to SA readers.

1980s

History

1980s   ANC resolves on 'urban insurgency' to 'make SA ungovernable'.
1983   Referendum on new constitution.
        United Democratic Front launched (non-racial).
1984+   Black school boycotts.
        Strikes.
        Urban insurgency.
        Emergency.
        Boycotts, marches, mass funerals.
        Widespread killings.
        12,000 detained (state figure).

Summary: Mass support for ANC; nationwide insurgency; rejection of reforms; political mobilisation and armed struggle; [Rhodesia: 1980 – landslide victory for Mugabe, independent Zimbabwe declared].

Texts

Canopus (1979–82); *Somers* (1983); *GT* (1985); *FC* (1988).

Final rejection of group endeavour in favour of personal compassion (especially feminist, pacifist and insurgent ideas and strategies). Entrenches role of author as sage.

Reviews

Reviews dry up completely, though Lessing's 'fame' is still followed. Current output seen as irrelevant to SA readers. Lessing is taken up by academics as an interesting and symptomatic 'colonial' author on the basis of her 'African' texts.

Appendix B

Anon. (Review of *The Grass Is Singing*), *Rand Daily Mail*, 11 March 1950.

Anon. (Review of *The Grass Is Singing*), *Cape Times*, 25 March 1950.

Anon. (Review of *The Grass Is Singing*) 'Novel that was neglected in S.A.', Johannesburg *Star*, 26 March 1950.

Anon. (Review of *The Grass Is Singing*) 'White Defeat in Africa: Gifted Young Woman's Bitter Novel about Rhodesia', *Star*, 17 April 1950.

Anon. (Review of *This Was the Old Chief's Country*) 'Doris Lessing's New Stories Take the Lid off Africa', *Star*, 12 April 1951.

Anon. (Review of *Martha Quest*) 'Doris Lessing Begins a Saga', *Star*, 22 January 1953.

Anon. (Review of *A Proper Marriage*) 'Martha Quest in the Throes of Marriage', *Star*, 11 November 1954.

Anon. (Reviews of *Retreat from Innocence*) 'Rhodesian Authoress Not Allowed To Enter SA Tells of her Political and Racial Dilemmas', *Sunday Times* (Johannesburg), 15 April 1956.

Anon. (Review of *Retreat from Innocence*) 'Doris Lessing Deserts the Veld for London', *Star*, 13 April 1956.

Anon. (Review of *Going Home*) 'Communist Doris Lessing Writes Book Attacking the Federation', *Rhodesian Herald* (Salisbury), 2 May 1957.

Anon. (Review of *Mr Dolinger*) 'Greed, Drink and Lust in Play about Rhodesian Life', *Argus* (Cape Town), 10 July 1958.

Anon. (Review of *Mr Dolinger*) 'Mrs Lessing Writes a Farcical Drama', *Rhodesian Herald* (Salisbury), 14 July 1958.

Anon. (Review of *The Truth about Billy Newton*) 'Doris Lessing's New Play Displeases', *Rhodesian Herald* (Salisbury), 20 January 1960.

Anon. (Reviews of *Play with a Tiger*) 'Superb Acting in Lessing Play', Johannesburg *Star*, 20 February 1962.

Anon. (Review of *Play with a Tiger*) 'Critics Skin This Tiger', Johannesburg *Star*, 23 March 1962.

Anon. (Review of *Golden Notebook*) 'The 4 Notebooks of Anna: Lessing Appears in Wulf's Clothing', Johannesburg *Star*, 24 May 1962.

Anon. (Review of *Four-Gated City*) 'Something Agley from Mrs Lessing', *Rand Daily Mail*, 5 September 1969.

Anon. (Review of *Briefing for a Descent into Hell*) 'Inner-Space Table of Loss of Memory', *Sunday Times*, 2 May 1971.

Barry, C. (Review of *Briefing for a Descent into Hell*), *Rand Daily Mail*, 2 July 1971.

Bernstein, Edgar. (Review of *The Grass is Singing*) 'A Notable SA Novel', *Trek* (Johannesburg) May 1950.

Baines, Nancy. [Untitled], *Cape Times*, 27 June 1962.

Cooper, A. A. 'Sci-fi Setting Fails', *Argus*, 11 June 1981.

Cope, R. K. (Jack). 'A Stark Life', *Cape Times*, 10 November 1954.

——. (Review of *A Ripple from the Storm*) 'Doris Lessing in Search of Herself', *Argus*, 10 December 1958.

Delius, Anthony. (Review of *The Grass Is Singing*) 'A Study in Black and White', *Standpunte*, 5.3 March 1951.

——. (Review of *Martha Quest*) 'Danger from the Digit', *Standpunte*, 7.3 April 1953.

Driver, C. J. (Jonty). 'The African-ness Holds these Stores Together', *Star*, 19 May 1973.

Foxe-Pitt, Cdr. 'Going Home', *Africa South*, 2.1 October 1957.

Gordimer, Nadine. (Review of *The Habit of Loving*), *Africa South*, 2.4 July 1958.

Israel, Norine. (Review of *Four-Gated City*) 'Prophetic Novel by Doris Lessing', *Cape Times*, 1 October 1969.

——. (Review of *Briefing for a Descent into Hell*) 'Inner Space Fiction', *Cape Times*, 23 June 1971.

——. (Review of *Summer before the Dark*) 'The Burden of Femininity', *Cape Times*, 25 May 1973.

Laski, Marghanita. (Review of *Grass Is Singing*), *Spectator* (London), 184 (31 March 1950).

Lewis, Peter. (Review of *Collected African Stories*) 'I'm Addicted . . . and This is Why', *Rand Daily Mail*, 29 March 1973.

Marais, David. (Review of *Going Home*) 'Disturbing Lens on Africa', *Argus*, 17 July 1957.

Morphet, Tony. (Review of *Sirian Experiments*) 'Doris Lessing Sticks to the Same Old Theme', *Sunday Times*, 18 August 1980.

Nkosi, Lewis. (Review of *Landlocked*) 'Les Grandes Dames', *New African*, 4.7 September 1965.

R. R. '*The Golden Notebook*', *Purple Renoster*, May 1963.

Randall, Peter. (Review of *Collected African Stories*) 'A Feast of Doris Lessing', *Rand Daily Mail*, 11 June 1976.

Snow, C. P. (Review of *Martha Quest*) 'Frustration on the Veldt', *Sunday Times* (London), 4 November 1950, p. 11.

Thompson, John. 'The Habit of Loving', *Cape Times*, 11 December 1957.

Walker, Oliver. (Review of *Going Home*) 'Novelist Given a Tarred White Feather in Bulawayo', *Star*, 26 June 1957.

Webster, Mary. (Review of *African Stories*) 'Fine Lessing Tales of Africa', *Sunday Times,* 19 July 1964.

W., M.M. [Mary Morrison Webster]. (Review of *Four-Gated City*) 'Doris Lessing Sees Only Gloom Ahead', *Cape Times*, 1 June 1969.

——. (Review of *This Was the Old Chief's Country*), *Sunday Times*, 27 May 1951.

W.J.P.B. [*sic*]. (Review of *Grass is Singing*) 'Writer's Grim Story of an African Farm', *Rand Daily Mail*, 11 March 1950.

3

Doris Lessing in Pursuit of the English, or, No Small, Personal Voice*

CLARE HANSON

Doris Lessing is out of favour with English criticism, when English criticism takes account of her work at all. After the ecstatic reception of *The Grass Is Singing* in 1950 (an 'astonishing accomplishment' said no less a paper than the *Daily Telegraph*) it has been downhill all the way, a textbook case of critics taking their own bafflement and confusion and reflecting it back on to the author. For example, in a long, anonymous review of *The Golden Notebook* in the *Times Literary Supplement* (*TLS*) in 1962, the (?male) critic concluded:

> There is no breaking of forms but an inability to impose form at all: the level of consciousness in all the notebooks is the same and very often the subject-matter overlaps, so that the reader cannot remember whether certain incidents are supposed to be fiction or fact . . . Her material has got badly out of hand, and in desperation she has bundled the lot together and chucked it at the reader to make of it what he [sic] can. (p. 280)

An exemplary case of a critic inadvertently hitting some nails on the head while labouring otherwise under a fog of incomprehension. After the critical reception accorded *The Golden Notebook* and *The Four-Gated City*, it is hardly surprising to find that Lessing's 'space fiction' found even fewer admirers in England: by this stage (the 1970s and 1980s), Lessing has become an open target. A *TLS* review of *The Sirian Experiments*, for example, begins,

* This essay is a complete and up-dated version of the paper delivered at MLA in 1986. A shorter version under the same title was published in *PN Review*, no. 60, 14:4 (January 1988): 39–42.

magisterially, 'Doris Lessing employs the science fiction genre purposefully, but not well', and the critic then goes on, interestingly, to attack Lessing's style: 'misplaced participles abound, singulars and plurals are confused, sentences are made verbless quite unnecessarily and there is much too much reliance on those magic triple dots' (Morgan, p. 431). (Critics seem to be in agreement that we don't read Lessing for the 'style', but, if at all, for the 'content'). There is general agreement too, it seems, that Lessing is now no longer aware of what *she's* doing: there is a nicely comic juxtaposition in the *TLS* of 3 June 1983 of a review of *The Sentimental Agents* in which it is claimed that Lessing is 'no longer capable' of seeing the irony of her position as an ex-colonial writing of a benevolent imperialism – and an advertisement below for *The Diary of a Good Neighbour* by Jane Somers – 'Likeable, readable and often funny, with good points to make and a warm heart at the centre of them' – so Isobel Quigley endorses *this* book (Wallis, p. 562)!

So much for the general critical reception (though obviously there have been critics who have responded more positively to what Lessing was trying to do, and there was in particular a noticeable warming of the critical temperature for *The Memoirs of a Survivor*). In specifically academic circles Lessing has been, as Claire Sprague has surmised, very largely ignored: it is quite extraordinary how invisible her work is beside that of Muriel Spark, for example, who had the good fortune to attract the attention of an influential male critic (Frank Kermode, ex-King Edward VII Professor of English Literature at Cambridge). It is quite clearly a question of *relative* neglect, as comparison with Spark, or with the younger Margaret Drabble, will show – it is not simply a question of the English academic establishment's well-known reluctance to engage with contemporary literature (there are no academic journals in England quite like *Modern Fiction Studies, Contemporary Literature* or *Twentieth-Century Literature*, remember). But, again, there are exceptions, though it has to be said that the bulk of the good work has been done by women critics, most notably in the only two serious book-length studies to date: Lorna Sage's (1983) excellent book in the Methuen Contemporary Writers Series, and Jenny Taylor's equally excellent collection of essays, *Notebooks/Memoirs/ Archives: Reading and Rereading Doris Lessing*. Ruth Whittaker, too, has just brought out a book-length study of Lessing with Macmillan.

The only two mainstream academic pieces I can trace by men are Patrick Parrinder's acute article on Lessing's later fiction in

Critical Quarterly in 1980, and an article by David Craig, also in *Critical Quarterly*, in 1984. The latter raises some of the issues I want particularly to explore in relation to Lessing's reception in England. It is a lucid and convincing piece, ingeniously linking together Lessing's *The Summer Before the Dark* (1972) and David Storey's *Pasmore* (1974). Craig sees these two novels as reflecting: 'the slump in middle-class morale in the 1970s, and, beneath that, a long-standing anxiety on the part of well-to-do Western people as their way of life has ceased to have a seemingly guaranteed and invulnerable basis' (p. 4). *The Summer Before the Dark* is one of those books which is: 'speaking authentically for a class or classes . . . expressing, dramatising or figuring the patterns of behaviour in which we do find ourselves moving in our own place and time' (Craig, p. 3). I think that Craig's view is mistaken but that it stems from a misconception which runs right through English criticism of Lessing's work. The English response to Lessing has been vitiated by a false perception of what she is about — and it is a false perception which has been largely created by Lessing herself. In her almost too well-known essay 'The Small Personal Voice' (1957), I suggest Lessing perpetrated a hoax on her public almost on the scale of the Jane Somers one. In this essay (written *after A Proper Marriage*), Lessing presents herself as above all a humanist realist. She writes:

> For me the highest point of literature was the novel of the nineteenth century, the work of Tolstoy, Stendhal, Dostoevsky, Balzac, Turgenev, Chekhov; the work of the great realists . . . I hold the view that the realist novel, the realist story, is the highest form of prose writing; higher than and out of the reach of any comparison with expressionism, impressionism, symbolism, naturalism, or any other ism. The great men of the nineteenth century had neither religion nor politics nor aesthetic principles in common. But what they did have in common was a climate of ethical judgement; they shared certain values; they were humanists.   (*SPV*, pp. 4–5)

In reading the great nineteenth-century realists she was looking for: 'the warmth, the compassion, the humanity, the love of people which illuminates the literature of the nineteenth century and which makes all these old novels a statement of faith in man himself' (*SPV*, p. 6). Lessing puts herself here in the liberal–

humanist tradition – taking into account and accommodating, as she must, the Lukacsian, Marxist point of view, but coming down, ultimately, in favour of the irreducible virtue and value of the individual: 'The point of rest should be the writer's recognition of man, the responsible individual, voluntarily submitting his will to the collective, but never finally' (*SPV*, p. 12). In stressing individual freedom in England in 1957 Lessing is very much of her place and time: this is the period of the 'angry young men' whose work Lessing describes in the same essay as 'an injection of vitality into the withered arm of British literature' (p. 15). It is also the time of John Bayley and Iris Murdoch's extremely influential polemics on behalf of the English novel; they prescribed, specifically, a programme of learning from realist tradition and of striving to depict 'free, separate characters'.

So it is easy to fit Lessing's essay into its historical context, but harder to relate it to the novels she was actually writing in this period. I don't think the cosy figure she presents – the 'gentle re-reader' of Tolstoy and Balzac – has very much to do with the strained texture of *A Proper Marriage*, for example. I would argue that Lessing was never a realist in the sense she suggests in 'The Small Personal Voice'. The essay was in effect a piece of camouflage, which served the useful purpose of pointing critics in the wrong direction, leaving Lessing free to pursue her own (devious) paths.

To suggest that Lessing – weighty Lessing, author of such enjoyably dense, long novels – is not 'really' a realist is to go right against the English critical grain, and to hit on a particular nerve. For in England: 'Respect for the tradition of the realist novel is apparently a very rooted fact, and is inextricably involved in a very complex set of responses to the decline of religion and the substitution of a Religion of Humanity' (Byatt, p. 21). Yet, surely, we are misreading a major modern novelist because of this 'very rooted fact'.[1]

There is not space here to examine Lessing's whole *oeuvre* in order to prove the point about realism, but we can look at key texts, for example, *The Four-Gated City*. This novel opens in an extremely diffident, muted way: it doesn't even exhibit the degree of commitment demanded by socialist realism, let alone the commitment (or 'love') demanded by 'realism' in an English context. Note the distanced, pseudo-scientific terms Lessing uses to describe the interior of a cafe in the opening paragraphs:

In front of Martha was grimed glass, its *lower part* covered with grimed muslin. The open door showed *an oblong* of browny-grey air swimming with *globules* of wet. The shop fronts opposite were no particular colour. The lettering on the shops, once black, brown, gold, white, was now shades of dull brown. The lettering *on the upper part* of the glass of this room said *Joe's Fish and Chips* in reverse, and was flaking like stale chocolate.

She sat by *a rectangle* of pinkish oilcloth where sugar had spilled, and on to it, orange tea, making a gritty smear in which someone had doodled part of a name: *Daisy Flet* . . . Her cup was thick whitey-grey, cracked. The teaspoon was a whitish plastic, so much used that the *elastic brittleness* natural to it had gone into an *erosion* of hair lines, so that it was like *a kind of sponge.* (*FGC*, p. 13; my italics)

A few pages into the novel, Lessing dramatises her own complex relationship to her 'factual' or 'real' material, via the characters of Martha Quest and Iris. In a striking passage she describes their double vision of England, veering between the twin poles of alienation and love:

She [Iris] knew everything about this area, half a dozen streets for about half a mile or a mile of their length; and she knew it all in such detail that when with her, *Martha walked in a double vision, as if she were two people: herself and Iris, one eye stating, denying, warding off the total hideousness of the whole area, the other, with Iris, knowing it in love. With Iris, one moved here, in state [sic] of love, if love is the delicate but total acknowledgement of what is.* Passing a patch of bared wall where the bricks showed a crumbling smear of mushroom colour, Iris was able to say: Mrs Black painted this wall in 1938, it was ever such a nice pink. Or: looking up at a lit window, the curtains drawn across under the black smear of the blackout material which someone had not got around to taking down: Molly Smith bought those curtains down at the market the first year of the war, before things got so scarce. Or, walking around a block in the pavement, she muttered that the workmen never seemed to be able to get that piece in square, she always stubbed her foot against it. Iris, Joe's mother, had lived in this street since she was born. Put her brain, together with the other million brains, women's brains, that recorded in such tiny loving anxious detail the histories of windowsills, skins of paint, replaced curtains and salvaged baulks of timber, there would be a recording instrument, a sort of six-dimensional map which included the histories and lives and loves of people, London – a section map in depth.　(*FGC*, p. 21; my italics)

This is an extremely important passage. In it, paradoxically, Lessing puts the case for realism more eloquently even than Murdoch – the case, that is, for a realism based on the concept of knowledge through love. But even stronger is the sense Lessing conveys of how *im*possible this kind of knowledge is for Martha – exiled, alienated Martha. For Martha, and by implication for Lessing herself, the 'other eye' is always 'stating' something else – qualifying, opening up different possibilities. There is, always, too much to know, and correspondingly no conceivable guarantee that one could ever know anything enough. Iris's (and Murdoch's!) kind of love is based on what the philosopher Hans Vaihinger would call a necessary fiction, a belief in the possibility of knowledge which is as it were self-enabling – but it is a belief which is utterly denied the Martha–Lessing figure with her stereoscopic, or multiscopic, vision.

In consequence of this epistemological uncertainty Lessing retreats increasingly in her fiction away from realism as the English understand it. I think the retreat begins at least as early as *A Proper Marriage*, though one could argue that there is a good deal of unease even in *The Grass Is Singing*, the prototypical 'realist' Lessing novel, in the conventional view. From the time of *The Golden Notebook* and *The Four-Gated City*, certainly, Lessing withdraws behind borrowed voices and masks – and I'd like to stress that it is very much a case of 'voices', of style, of language. It is a very English blindness not to see how important style is for Lessing – see, for example, Anne Duchêne, in a 1978 *TLS* review of the *Collected Stories* in which she states that we read Lessing for what she says, not for the way she says it (p. 695). This blindness, or deafness, to the question of style contributes a good deal to the English misreading of her work.

At one point in *The Golden Notebook* Anna Wulf reflects on the impossibility of making 'stories' fit 'the truth':

Yet now what interests me is precisely this – why did I not write an account of what had happened, instead of shaping a 'story' which had nothing to do with the material that fuelled it. Of course, the straight, simple, formless account would not have been a 'novel' and would not have got published, but I was genuinely not interested in 'being a writer' . . . I am simply asking myself: Why a story at all — not that it was a bad story, or untrue, or that it debased anything. Why not, simply, the truth?   (pp. 81–2)

What is true for stories is true also for style: Lessing (like other post-modernist writers) is obsessed by the fact of the falsity of her medium. Words are always secondhand, 'stale' as she puts it, tainted by innumerable other possible contexts: the same is true of styles, i.e. ways of connecting words. Lessing employs an extraordinarily wide range of styles in her fiction, shifting from, for example, the register of documentary to that of romantic fiction to that of social satire. The frequency with which she switches styles needs to be stressed, as does the fact that she takes the relativist position in relation to style about as far as one can go in the preface to *The Diaries of Jane Somers*. Here she suggests that, even if we were to concede that there is some kind of 'ground note' linking together all the different styles employed by 'Doris Lessing', it is a ground note which she, the historical, 'actual' woman Doris Lessing, can change at will, when she chooses to write as 'Jane Somers':

And it did turn out that as Jane Somers I wrote in ways that Doris Lessing cannot. It was more than a question of using the odd turn of phrase or an adjective to suggest a woman journalist who is also a successful romantic novelist: Jane Somers knew nothing about a kind of dryness, like a conscience, that monitors Doris Lessing whatever she writes and in whatever style. (*DJS*,   Preface)

This acute sense of the relativity of style accounts for the many occasions in Lessing's fiction when one of her writer–narrator figures hesitates before a choice of words or a choice of style: Lessing foregrounds the moment of crisis before commitment, and the gap, the space before commitment, is the nearest approximation we can have to 'the truth' which in truth no words or style can compass.

The use of different styles is usually presented as very much a matter of choice and of determination. However, on occasion in Lessing's fiction, the adoption of another person's voice is presented as something over which (the writer) has no conscious control. Does language 'speak' us, as much as we speak language?

> At which my mind slipped into a gear foreign to me, and I began writing a story about June Boothby. I was unable to stop the flow of words, and I was in tears of frustration as I wrote in the style of the most insipid coy women's magazine; but what was frightening was that the insipidity was due to a very slight alteration of my own style, a word here and there only.   (*GN*, p. 597)

To summarise the argument so far: I would suggest that, in contradiction to the prevailing English view, Doris Lessing is not a realist novelist who, after some aberration and dallying with 'science fiction', is returning to the realist fold with the Jane Somers novels and *The Good Terrorist*. I would argue that Lessing is a far, far more radical writer than this, one whose work reflects almost every possible stage and process in the 'dehumanisation of art' and of the individual in the post-humanist world. Her work should be seen as post-modern and post-humanist, and placed in the context of the theory of critics such as Julia Kristeva and Jacques Derrida, and the practice of writers such as Mario Vargas Llosa, Clarice Lispector, Italo Calvino. To put it another way: the English try to parochialise Lessing when she is the last writer we should try to do this to. Her work belongs, most saliently, to the international, transcultural marketplace of post-modern art.

One example, to support the argument: take Lessing's distrust of styles, her mixing of styles, and her exploration of the slippery path leading 'down' from art to the style of romantic fiction in parts of *The Golden Notebook*. Lessing's stance, her view of language is very like that of Mario Vargas Llosa in *Aunt Julia and the Scriptwriter* (Picador, 1984): there is exactly the same sense of the relativity of style and – a point I haven't previously pressed – the same implicit questioning of the boundaries between 'high' and 'low' art, the 'style' of art and that of the magazine.

We should now, then, see Lessing as a particular kind of sage or seer: an 'ancient wom[a]n/Gathering fuel in vacant lots', a literary scavenger in a post-humanist void – only working, unlike Eliot, in the humanist *form* of the novel – hence 'much confusion'.

The English misreading of Lessing has been due to a very English refusal to acknowledge both her bleakness, and her wit and sophistication – a case of deep-rooted resistance to experiment outside the liberal–humanist tradition. It is rather depressing to see that a similar resistance to experiment has marred the English feminist response to Lessing over the last few years, so that English feminists seem to have missed out, most crucially, on what Lessing has been trying to do with gender and gender-expectations in her space fiction. Here it would seem to be a case of deep-rooted mistrust of any departure from the Marxist–feminist model of women's oppression. Because Lessing has moved away from this kind of analysis to a kind of 'play' with gender which fits more closely into the European post-feminist framework of Julia Kirsteva and Luce Irigaray, she seems largely to have lost the sympathy and interest of English feminist critics. I have been able to trace very little work done by English feminist critics on Lessing's play with gender in the space fiction:[2] this means that a crucial departure in Lessing's *oeuvre* has gone 'quite underground' in England. Lessing's role as one of the female fantasists of the 1970s in England (others include Angela Carter, Beryl Bainbridge, Fay Weldon) has similarly gone unnoticed and unacknowledged.

Just one example of the poor reception of Lessing's 'female fantasy' in her space fiction. *The Marriages Between Zones Three, Four, and Five* offers itself as an obvious example of a text which feminist critics might have focused on and elucidated. Yet the book was reviewed (inevitably?) by a male critic in the *TLS*, who actually got away with calling it a 'radiant epithalamium' (Korn, p. 520). There has thus been in England tacit acceptance (not so tacit in the case of students) of the notion that in this novel Lessing was *celebrating* gender difference as we know it today. This is, of course, not the case. In *The Marriages* Lessing first short-circuits gender politics by positing a new kind of communion existing *only* between members of the same sex (Al·Ith and Dabeeb): she then gestures towards a desire to transcend gender difference at the end of the novel. Gender difference has provided interest, meaning (and pleasure) for Al·Ith in the past, but she seems to move at the close of the novel beyond gender difference, perhaps difference itself, as the primary ground and constituent of meaning.

In moving beyond bourgeois humanism and contemporary sexual politics in her writing Lessing has far outdistanced the English of whom she once, disingenuously, declared herself to be

in pursuit. To bring the story up to date: the reception of the Jane
Somers novels and of *The Good Terrorist* has been fairly stormy,
which is cheering as it suggests a response greater than indifference
to the later Lessing. Via the Jane Somers hoax Lessing boldly
challenged the system by means of which literary value and worth
is established in England: the success of her deception and of her
challenge has far-reaching implications. Can we ever again ignore
the ways in which reader-expectations, themselves manufactured
by (not disinterested) critics, manufacture and create the 'texts'
which we read? Quite apart from the overall manner of *presentation*
of the Jane Somers novels, their *style*, too, opens up questions
about the creation of literary value and meaning. In the Jane
Somers novels Lessing experiments with style in a specific way,
playing in particular with the boundaries between 'good' and 'bad'
style as she had with Anna Wulf in *The Golden Notebook*. It is, as
she says in the preface to *Diaries*, 'more than a question of using
the odd turn of phrase or an adjective to suggest a woman journalist
who is also a successful romantic novelist' – in toying with
'bad' art, magazine style, the style of romantic fiction, Lessing
disconcerts/deconstructs 'her' reader, and forces us to see the
relative and perhaps arbitrary ways in which 'value' is constructed.

The Good Terrorist received fairly lukewarm reviews in the general
press, but was forcefully attacked by both male and female critics
on the left. Their thesis has been that in this novel Lessing has
finally given up: the ex-radical has sunk into the clichés of suburban
fascism (back to the *Daily Telegraph*). Such critics view Lessing's
presentation of cliché-ridden (and driven) Alice Mellings in *The
Good Terrorist* as by definition an *attack* on Alice, and see Lessing
as endorsing the opinions of Alice's mother, the representative of
the older generation:

> I'll tell you something, Zoe. All you people, marching up and
> down and waving banners and singing pathetic little songs – all
> you need is love; you are just a joke. To the people who really
> run this world, you are a joke. They watch you at it and think:
> Good, that's keeping them busy.   (p. 335)

says Dorothy Mellings to the friend who has not yet given up all
the accoutrements of radicalism. But surely the point is that *all* the
characters in *The Good Terrorist* are clichéd, are stereotyped, perhaps
especially Dorothy. In this novel, Lessing presents us with

something rather like Joyce's 'tired style' towards the end of *Ulysses*. The book is, I would argue, composed of dead language, finished language, stereotyped and clichéd language, which seems to construct the characters rather than the characters constructing it. *The Good Terrorist* is a grey and textureless novel because it is 'about' or speaks, a grey and textureless language: it is, surely, quite missing the point to see the drabness as the symptom of authorial laziness (the idea here being that we are given an inadequate and 'faulty' realism – Lessing just can't be bothered any more to describe the inside of a squat properly).

In *The Good Terrorist* Lessing gives us not a literature but a language of exhaustion. It is a bleak book because it is not only presenting us with the issue of the relativity of style but presenting us too with the spectacle of language winding down, receiving no new impetus or energy from any single individual. Specifically, it is a question of a loss of faith in the power and potential of the individual, a loss of belief in the 'small, personal voice'. In questioning the construct of the individual and in challenging our concepts of identity and self-presence, Lessing in her later work belongs fully to the post-modern tradition. In her writing she challenges both the authority of identity and the identity of the author, with consequences for both content *and* form. The form of her work becomes increasingly open, problematic, often rough and unresolved. (I would argue that the form of *The Good Terrorist*, for example, is unresolved: the narrative is truncated and the style uncertain – there is no *aesthetic* comfort here.) The situation in Lessing's work is now very like that described by Jean-François Lyotard in *The Postmodern Condition*. He characterises post-modern art in this way:

> The postmodern would be that which, in the modern, puts forward the unpresentable in presentation itself; that which denies itself the solace of good forms, the consensus of a taste which would make it possible to share collectively the *nostalgia*[3] for the unattainable; that which searches for new presentations, not in order to enjoy them but in order to impart a stronger sense of the unpresentable. A postmodern artist or writer is in the position of a philosopher: the text he writes, the work he produces are not in principle governed by preestablished rules, and they cannot be judged according to a determining judgement, by applying familiar categories to the text or to the work.

Those rules and categories are what the work of art itself is looking for. (p. 81)[4]

Notes

1. Here are two examples of the English stress on Lessing's 'realism': 'In fact, the authenticity of [Doris Lessing's] writing, the conviction that these are lives really being lived recognisably in our time, the extraordinary assurance and precision with which from the very first her characters were presented and the world in which they moved, were the qualities which put her straight away among the most powerful writers of the postwar generation' ('The Fog of War', p. 280); 'The Coldriges are a marvellous creation, a splendid, many tentacled family whose teas and house-parties manage to kaleidoscope the entire social and political geography of postwar Britain. Mark's mother, Tory hostess and patroness of the arts, brings luncheon hampers to the Aldermaston marchers of 1958, where her extraordinary, typically English family are assembled on the fringe of Hyde Park' (Raban, p. 112).
2. The most interesting essay, Marsha Rowe's 'If You Mate a Swan and a Gander, Who Will Ride', is collected in Taylor. The issue of gender is also touched on in a suggestive article by Sage (1986), 'The Available Space'.
3. Lessing too repeatedly uses the word 'nostalgia' in connection with a too-easy pleasure in art. See, for example, *The Golden Notebook*, the last paragraph of the first 'black notebook'.
4. Since this essay was written, Lessing has published a book on the war in Afghanistan, *The Wind Blows Away Our Words* (1987), which I have discussed elsewhere as an 'invaded' text (Hanson, 1988). She has also published *The Fifth Child* (1988), a text which takes further what is surely emerging as central to Lessing's work, her critique of humanism. In this wonderful and appalling novel Lessing forces us to confront head-on the question of the essentiality of humanity and of human(e) values. In creating the rejected mutant, Ben, she is able to play with the whole idea of 'humanity': the novella is structured around the paradox that it is because Ben is 'outside the human limit' that his supposedly 'civilised' (i.e. humane) society inhumanely rejected him. Is it merely coincidence that in hitting on this illustrative metaphor to reflect her deepest concerns, Lessing seems to find her voice, or her 'best' voice in fiction since *The Memoirs of a Survivor*? The prose of *The Fifth Child* is marvellously spare, supple and exact. Predictably, but still shockingly, *The Fifth Child* was not even shortlisted in England for the prestigious Booker Prize of 1988.

Works Cited

Bayley, John. *The Characters of Love*. London: Constable, 1960.

Byatt, A. S. 'People in Paper Houses: Attitudes to "Realism" and "Experiment" in English Postwar Fiction'. *Stratford-upon-Avon Studies 18: The Contemporary English Novel*. Ed. Malcolm Bradbury and David Palmer. London: Edward Arnold, 1978. pp. 19–41.

Craig, David. 'Middle-class Tragedy'. *Critical Quarterly* 26.3 (1984): 3–19.

Duchêne, Anne. 'The Steps to the Pulpit'. *Times Literary Supplement* 22 (June 1978): 695.

'The Fog of War'. *Times Literary Supplement* 27 April 1962: 280.

Hanson, Clare. Review of *The Wind Blows Away Our Words* by Doris Lessing. *Doris Lessing Newsletter* 12.1 (Spring 1988): 8–9.

Korn, Eric. 'Al·Ith in Wonderland'. *Times Literary Supplement* 9 May 1980: 520.

Lessing, Doris. *The Four-Gated City*. London: Macgibbon & Kee, 1969.

——. *The Golden Notebook*. St Albans: Panther, 1973.

——. *A Small Personal Voice; Essays, Reviews, Interviews*, ed. Paul Schlueter. New York: Knopf, 1974.

——. *The Diaries of Jane Somers*. London: Michael Joseph, 1984.

——. *The Fifth Child*. London: Jonathan Cape, 1988.

Lyotard, Jean-François. *The Postmodern Condition: A Report on Knowledge*. Tr. Geoff Bennington and Brian Massumi. Manchester: Manchester University Press, 1984.

Morgan, Edwin. 'Empire of the Stars'. *Times Literary Supplement* 17 April 1981: 431.

Murdoch, Iris. 'Against Dryness'. *Encounter* 16 (January 1961): 16–20.

Parrinder, Patrick. 'Descents into Hell: The Later Novels of Doris Lessing'. *Critical Quarterly* 22.4 (1980): 5–25.

Quigley, Isobel. From a review cited in an advertisement for *The Diary of Jane Somers*. *Times Literary Supplement* 3 June 1983.

Raban, Jonathan. 'Mrs Lessing's Diary'. *London Magazine* 9.6 (September 1969): 111–15.

Sage, Lorna. *Doris Lessing*. London: Methuen, 1983.

——. 'The Available Space'. *Women's Writing*. Ed. Moira Monteith. Brighton: Harvester Press, 1986. 15–33.

Taylor, Jenny, ed. *Notebooks/Memoirs/Archives: Reading and Rereading Doris Lessing*. London: Routledge & Kegan Paul, 1982.

Wallis, F. L. 'Rhetorical Diseases' [Review of *The Sentimental Agents*]. *Times Literary Supplement* 3 June 1983: p. 562.

4

From Supermarket to Schoolroom: Doris Lessing in the United States

ELLEN CRONAN ROSE

Doris Lessing has been a figure in the intellectual landscape of the United States since 1962, when the *New York Times* greeted *The Golden Notebook* as a 'coruscating literary event' (Buckler). Though she had by that time written five novels, three collections of short stories, two autobiographical narratives, a book of poems and a play, only four of these books had been published in the United States: *The Grass Is Singing, This Was the Old Chief's Country, The Habit of Loving* and *In Pursuit of the English*. American reviewers of *This Was the Old Chief's Country* presented Lessing as 'one of the most talented younger British writers of the last decade' (Peden, 1952), whose 'further development . . . should be watched for' (Fitzgerald). Her second volume of short stories, *The Habit of Loving*, was seen as 'a first-class achievement by one of England's very best contemporary writers' (Peden, 1958), a woman who had 'slipped into the uneasy circle of England's Angry Young Men' (Peden, 1958).

This is standard 'reviewers' rhetoric', familiar to regular readers of the *New York Times Book Review* or the *Saturday Review*. It 'places' a writer for the literary/intellectual cognoscenti, validating a certain kind of cocktail- or dinner-party conversation. The language that described *The Golden Notebook* was something else again. Irving Howe said it was 'the most absorbing and exciting piece of new fiction' he had read 'in a decade', because 'it moves with the beat of our time, and it is true' (p. 181). In particular, he praised Lessing for creating in Anna Wulf 'that rarity in modern fiction . . . a mature intellectual woman' (p. 177). The 'center' of the book, for Howe, consisted of conversations between Anna and Molly in 'Free Women':

74

When they discuss their failures in love, their problems as divorced women with children to raise, their disillusionments as former Communists who would still like to needle the Establishment, their inability to talk with the passionless and apolitical young, their contempt for the new gentility of intellectual London, their difficulties in reconciling the image they hold of a self-sufficient human being with the needs they feel as anything but self-sufficient women – when these conversations between Anna and Molly recur throughout the book, one turns to them with the delight of encountering something real and fresh.   (pp. 178–9)

Howe praised Lessing for being 'radically different from other women writers who have dealt with the problems of their sex, first in that she grasps the connection between Anna Wulf's neuroses and the public disorders of the day, and second in that she has no use either for the quaverings of the feminist writers or the aggressions of those female novelists whose every sentence leads a charge in the war of the sexes' (p. 178). The accuracy of Howe's perception is confirmed by Lessing's 1971 preface to a new edition of *The Golden Notebook*, in which she testily denied that she wrote it as 'a tract about the sex war' (Lessing, 1973, p. x).

Nevertheless, as Annis Pratt has observed, in 1962, 'when the new feminist movement was in its embryonic stages, Lessing's novel brought to consciousness a quality of being which she herself had taken "absolutely for granted"' (Pratt, p. 413). And because of 'its insistence on freedom, its moments of aggression [and] its attacks on the masculine world', by the end of the decade *The Golden Notebook* had been appropriated by many feminists as 'a document in the history of liberation' (Drabble, p. 188).

The feminism of the late sixties was the culmination of a decade of social protest. The civil rights movement, the anti-Vietnam movement and the women's movement were all radical in their determination to cut through the pious rhetoric of the Eisenhower fifties ('America is a land of opportunity where all are equal'; 'The US is a non-aggressive, non-imperialist democracy'; 'Woman's place is in the home') to the reality of racial, sexual and global exploitation. All three movements derived from the people (tenant farmers, suburban housewives, churchgoers), but assumed their characteristic shape in the university (SNCC, SDS, the free speech movement, women's studies programmes). For while the experience of exploitation belonged to common folk, its analysis seemed to demand the rigour of trained academicians. And when students and professors became active politically, politics had a way of sneaking into the academy.

In December 1968, a small band of political activists led by Louis Kampf and Paul Lauter staged a coup at the annual convention of the Modern Language Association (MLA). 'The Little Bourgeois Cultural Revolution of MLA 1968' (Kampf and Lauter, p. 34) succeeded in forcing the MLA to accommodate the demands of radicals, blacks, women and other minorities for more representation in its governance structure. But the militant professors wanted more than token representation of minority groups on the governing boards of the MLA; they also wanted to force the literary profession to re-examine its ideology, to 'explore the class biases, sexual biases, and ethnic biases in the structure of literature departments as well as in their operational definition, evaluation, and presentation of literature' (Franklin, pp. 94–5). 'By the mid 1950's', one of these revolutionaries wrote, 'almost the entire body of literature created and widely enjoyed by the peoples of America had been rejected [by the academy] in favor of an infinitesimal canon of "great" works by literary "masters", mostly professional white gentlemen not unlike those selecting them' (Franklin, p. 102).

One of the legacies of the 1968 MLA revolution was the establishment of a Commission on the Status of Women in the Profession, and in the seventies literary scholarship in this country was transformed by women who were both academics and feminists. Unable to reconcile their experience as women with the 'literature' they were taught as undergraduate and graduate students,[1] they rewrote course syllabi, freshman anthologies and PhD reading lists to represent what 'mattered' to them. For these women, as Annis Pratt recalls, the memorable thing about Lessing's Anna Wulf 'was not her ironic "freedom" but the fact that (after years of our attempts to identify ourselves with Quentin Compson, Augie March, and the Invisible Man, not to mention Lolita and Franny Glass) we were presented with a novel whose persona was an intellectual, a political activist, an artist, as well as a lover, a mother – a woman' (Pratt, p. 413).

Lessing's novels spoke with particular immediacy to those of us who were female graduate students in the late sixties and early seventies. What we discovered, when we read *The Golden Notebook* or the Martha Quest novels, was a writer who, it seemed, knew us better than we knew ourselves, who – as Anna Wulf would say – 'named' us and the welter of ambiguities in which we floundered. *This*, we felt, was what was lacking in our study and teaching of literature which, to those of us who had cut our teeth on Brooks and Warren's *Introduction to Poetry*, consisted of closely read 'texts' hermetically sealed from the mess we came home to every night. Doris Lessing 'is the kind of writer who changes people's lives', Margaret Drabble has said (p. 50). She certainly changed the professional lives of a significant number of academics, who battled their graduate advisors for permission to write their dissertations on Lessing, who risked their chances for tenure by writing articles and books on her, who daringly added *Martha Quest* to their seminar on the *Bildungsroman* or *The Golden Notebook* to a course in Modern British Fiction.

The initial US scholarship on Doris Lessing was written by men: James Gindin, Frederick Karl, Frederick P. W. McDowell, John Carey, Paul Schlueter. But after 1971, men as a class dropped out of Lessing scholarship. There were individual exceptions, of course: Frederick Karl's articles on *The Golden Notebook* and *The Four-Gated City*; John Carey's and Joseph Hynes's influential analyses of the structure of *The Golden Notebook*; Mark Spilka's comparative study of Lessing and Lawrence; Michael Magie's controversial essay on Lessing and romanticism. But from 1971 to 1986,[2] 78 per cent of the articles, 88 per cent of the books, 93 per cent of the MLA presentations and 95 per cent of the dissertations on Lessing in this country were written by women.

Mona Knapp observes, further, that 'in both scholarly and popular essays of the last fifteen years, it has become almost commonplace to initiate any discussion of modern feminist literature by mentioning *The Golden Notebook*' (p. 108). Chapters or sections on Lessing appear in some of the landmark books of feminist scholarship and criticism written over the past fifteen years: Patricia Meyer Spacks's *The Female Imagination* (1975), Sydney Janet Kaplan's *Feminine Consciousness in the Modern British Novel* (1975), Elaine Showalter's *A Literature of Their Own* (1977), Barbara Hill Rigney's *Madness and Sexual Politics in the Feminist Novel* (1978), Carol Christ's *Diving Deep and Surfacing* (1980), Lee R. Edwards's *Psyche as Hero* (1984) and Rachel Blau DuPlessis's *Writing Beyond the Ending* (1985).

It is, therefore, possible to study Lessing's 'reception' in the

United States as a paradigm of feminism's relationship to the academy from the early seventies to the present.

As I pointed out earlier, academic feminists read Lessing for the same reasons that their non-academic (white, middle-class) counterparts read her – because she articulated their experience. There is virtually no difference between the 'tone' of Marilyn Webb's 1973 article on Lessing in *The Village Voice* and Nancy Porter's in *World Literature Written in English*. Both authors invoke the first person. 'Before I read Doris Lessing I thought the women's movement was dead', Webb begins. But 'reading Lessing I remember what a woman's life is like' (p. 1). Porter was less grateful: 'I spent part of this past summer cabined with Doris Lessing; that is, with her writing. I must say I was not altogether happy with the way the affair went, with Lessing's insistent refusal to iron out the wrinkles in our commonality as women' (p. 161). Eventually, however, Porter acknowledged that Lessing had helped her recover 'in the images of time and place in *Children of Violence* and *The Golden Notebook* large portions of my past, as a woman and as a child of violence' (p. 179).

Having discovered writers who were personally meaningful to them, feminist academics – like their black colleagues – wanted to teach them, so that future generations of women and black students would not be crippled, as they felt they had been, by an education which made white, male, upper- and middle-class experience normative. While feminist literary historians worked to discover and publish 'lost' women writers of the past, those of us who primarily read contemporary authors had a different task – to validate 'popular' writers for serious academic study. Hence, while articles on Lessing as personal and political as Nancy Porter's continued to be written throughout the decade (e.g. Libby, Markow, Rapping), the principal aim of Lessing scholarship in the seventies was to get the academy to take Doris Lessing seriously.

In 1971, Doris Lessing took up one and a half column inches in the MLA Bibliography. There was one book on Lessing – Dorothy Brewster's 1965 volume in the Twayne series – and a chapter on her in James Gindin's *Postwar British Fiction* (1962). There were two scholarly articles – Frederick P. W. McDowell's 'The Fiction of Doris Lessing: An Interim View', in the 1965 volume of the *Arizona Quarterly*, and Selma Burkom's 'Only Connect: Form and Content in the Works of Doris Lessing', in the 1968 volume of *Critique*. McDowell had also devoted several pages to Lessing in two review essays on 'recent British fiction' in *Contemporary Literature*, as had Frederick Karl in *A Reader's Guide to the Contemporary English Novel* (1963), Walter Allen in *The Modern Novel in Britain and the United States* (1964) and Bernard Bergonzi in *The Situation of the Novel* (1970).

So it was rather daring of Paul Schlueter to petition the Modern Language Association that year for permission to convene a seminar on 'The Fiction of Doris Lessing'. However, more than forty Lessing enthusiasts assembled to hear papers read by Leonard Ashley, a Brooklyn College professor, and three young scholars, Selma Burkom, Lois Marchino and Diane Smith. Burkom and Smith had completed dissertations on Lessing in 1970 and 1971; Marchino's was still in progress.

In the discussion that followed, names were exchanged, addresses jotted down, and an informal but passionately dedicated exchange of letters, papers and support was set in motion. In 1976, after five years of Doris Lessing seminars at the MLA, Dee Seligman – who had completed a dissertation on Lessing in 1975 – founded the *Doris Lessing Newsletter* to 'facilitate the sharing of ideas and information among serious readers of Doris Lessing' (Statement 2). By the end of the decade, thirty-five 'serious readers' of Doris Lessing had entered the profession by way of a doctoral dissertation on her work. They and others had published five books on Lessing and seventy-three articles (twelve of them in a special number of *Contemporary Literature* devoted to Doris Lessing). They had met once a year at the Doris Lessing seminar at MLA and corresponded informally and in the pages of the *Newsletter*. And in 1979, they organised formally as the Doris Lessing Society, 'in order to maintain our presence at the MLA [as an Allied Organisation] and to insure the regular contact of those who are studying Lessing' ('Lessing Society').

The rest is history – *academic* history. Since 1980, when the new Allied Organisation convened two panels on Doris Lessing at the MLA Convention, scholarship on Lessing has become not only respectable but prolific. The decade began auspiciously with *Modern Fiction Studies'* special 'Doris Lessing Number' and drew to a close with three clear indications that the 'popular novelist' of the early sixties had been canonised 'an author'. In 1986, a volume on Lessing appeared in G. K. Hall's well-respected series, *Critical Essays on Modern British Literature* (Sprague and Tiger); also in 1986, the MLA's Committee on Teaching and Related Activities

authorised preparation of a volume on *The Golden Notebook* for the
MLA series, *Approaches to Teaching World Literature* (Kaplan and
Rose, 1989); and in 1987, a collection of papers on Lessing delivered
at MLA conventions between 1971 and 1985, prefaced by a critical
history of MLA Lessing scholarship, was awarded the Northeast
Modern Language Association/Ohio University Press prize for 'the
best book length manuscript on literary criticism or literary history
written in 1986 by a NEMLA member' (Kaplan and Rose, 1988).

But a funny thing happened on the way to the canon. Doris
Lessing stopped writing meaningfully for the general public. As
early as 1973, Florence Howe had predicted that 'when someone
writes the history of Lessing's life and work, that person will find
that sometime before or during the writing of *The Four-Gated City*'
a major 'shift' occurred in Lessing's preoccupations, from social
analysis and political commitment to 'an interest in Eastern thought'
and 'a belief in the mind (above and beyond material conditions)'
(Howe, 420). Writing in 1980 (the same year *Modern Fiction Studies*
honoured Lessing with a special number), political theorist and
feminist Jean Bethke Elshtain characterised Doris Lessing's 'post-
Golden Notebook' fiction as a 'repudiation of history' (p. 95). In *The
Four-Gated City*, *Briefing for a Descent into Hell*, *The Summer Before
the Dark* and *The Memoirs of a Survivor*, Elshtain charged, Lessing
had 'retreat[ed] from politics and the novel of social realism' (p. 95).
And 'as her contempt for the present and her eschatological
zeal have grown in scope and breadth, her fiction has become
increasingly remote and abstract, laced through with bitterness
and residues of regret, bespeaking a view of life turned sour, the
sourness of one who has tried the world and found it wanting'
(p. 96). Reading the fourth of Lessing's *Canopus* novels, *The Making
of the Representative for Planet 8*, convinced John Leonard that 'Mrs
Lessing is no longer very interested in people' (1982, p. 205) and –
true to human nature – people have responded by losing interest
in Doris Lessing.

While it is difficult, if not impossible, to prise sales figures out
of publishers,[3] it is possible to make some inferences from studying
Books in Print and *Books Out of Print*. Only one of Lessing's novels
is currently available in a mass-market paperback, the Bantam
Golden Notebook. In 1987, *The Four-Gated City*, which had been
available as a Bantam paperback, was temporarily out of print,
pending its reissue in the NAL Plume series, where it will join the

four preceding volumes of *Children of Violence*. Most of the rest of Lessing's books are Vintage paperbacks.

Undeniably these facts reflect recent mergers and acquisitions in the publishing industry. But they also probably reflect market research that tells publishers what audience to target for a particular book or author. Publishers have apparently concluded that Lessing's appeal, now, is primarily to academics. Plume and Vintage paperbacks are not only more expensive than the Bantam, Ballantine and Popular Library paperbacks in which Lessing was packaged in the seventies; they also have wide margins (convenient for note-taking) and are distributed not in supermarkets but in bookshops, principally though not exclusively in university bookshops.

Academics are professionally interested in novels for two reasons, to teach them and to write about them. At the end of the sixties, as I have suggested, a number of professors wanted to teach and write about novels that were both personally meaningful to them and that also spoke honestly and pertinently about the multifarious experiences ignored by the traditional literary canon. Publication of Doris Lessing's work, particularly *The Golden Notebook*, coincided with a moment in US cultural history when a generation of feminists attempted to reformulate the academic canon to represent the hitherto unrepresented experience of women. But that moment – when the distinction between the general or common reader and the academic was blurred – was fleeting.

Early criticism of Lessing, like much feminist criticism in the seventies, focused on the *content* of her novels, their compelling articulation of a mid-century malaise compounded of racial tension, the crisis in liberalism, sexual warfare and the breakdown of meaningful personal and familial relationships. In particular, this criticism applauded Lessing's 'accurate' depiction of women, especially in *The Golden Notebook*, a 'monumental achievement' that seemed to make some 'ultimate statement about twentieth-century women' (Showalter, 1977, p. 308). Feminist critics in the seventies concentrated on *The Golden Notebook* because it struck them as 'the most self-conscious and elaborate study, in imaginative terms, of the "free" woman's problems' in our literature (Spacks, p. 395). They combed its pages for both confirmation and analysis of their own problems, as ostensibly 'free' women, with identity, sexuality, politics and work.[4] Their methodology was primarily psychological; they 'analysed' Anna Wulf as if she were a living person – their sister.

But by the end of the decade, a second generation of American academic feminists – caught up in the prevailing fascination with continental post-structuralist theory – was calling this 'images of women' criticism naive.[5] It was pointless to look for images or representations of women in fiction because, these Lacanians, Derrideans and Foucaultians asserted, the self is constructed in and by language. Novels are not transparent windows opening on to 'reality', but elaborate verbal artifacts demanding deconstruction.

From 1980 on, Lessing criticism – like feminist criticism in general – has increasingly reflected continental post-structuralist literary theory, which deconstructs the form/content dichotomy by showing that 'content' is the result of certain linguistic 'deployments' and narrative 'strategies'. Accordingly, attention has shifted to the formal characteristics of Lessing's fiction, which is now typically approached by way of Saussurean linguistics, Derridean deconstruction and Roland Barthes's distinction between the *scriptible* and the *lisible*.[6]

If the prevailing mode of feminist criticism today, in the United States as in Europe, is linguistic and theoretical rather than political, it is reasonable to conclude that it is not primarily motivated by a desire to challenge the sterile professionalism of the academy. Elaine Showalter has recently charged that 'feminist criticism in general has moved inexorably, book by book, back into standard critical time' (1987, p. 40): 'In 1974, *Daniel Deronda* was read in radical feminist circles as a guide to living. . . . Since the late 1970s, though, feminist readings of *Daniel Deronda* show the impact of deconstruction [and] the theories of Lacan and Foucault' (pp. 40–1). The same, I suggest, might be said of *The Golden Notebook*. Showalter concludes her indictment of contemporary feminist criticism by quoting Gayatri Spivak's warning that we must be wary of the 'recuperation of the critical energies of feminism into the ruling ideology of Departments of English' and the possibility that this integration 'might involve compromises . . . that might not let a feminism survive' (1987, p. 42). John Guillory thinks that academic feminists' 'success' in revising the literary canon is not so much a 'victory of an oppositional culture' as a recuperation, by the academic establishment, of potentially disruptive energies (1987, p. 497). Put simply, the charge is that feminist criticism has been absorbed into the academic/literary 'mainstream'.

There seems to be an uncanny parallel between first- and second-generation feminist scholarship and what we might call first- and second-generation Lessing. No longer perceived as personally relevant by the general reader, the Lessing who authored the *Canopus in Argos* series is beloved alike by minimalist composer Philip Glass and post-structuralist feminist critics who reread *The Golden Notebook* as post-modernist fiction.[7]

But, *pace* Showalter, Spivak and Guillory, not all academic feminists have been 'recuperated' by the academy. Now, as in the early seventies, many academic feminists of both sexes add *The Golden Notebook* to their syllabi in order to raise political and ideological issues, not in order to compare it to *Tristram Shandy* or *The Counterfeiters* as an example of a 'self-consuming artifact' or metafiction. What they have to contend with is a generation of 'post-feminist' students who read it as a curious, interesting, but finally irrelevant historical document. Roberta Rubenstein, one of the Lessing scholars whose work did much to validate Lessing for academic attention, taught *The Golden Notebook* in an introductory course in Women's Studies because, for her, it is 'one of the most profound explorations of a woman's complex consciousness that exists in fiction' (p. 72). For Rubenstein, as for many of us who read, reread, write about and teach *The Golden Notebook*, the novel matters because it seems to record a chapter of our own history. Anna is 'a hero of our time' and *The Golden Notebook* 'a central text that articulate[s] our own experiences as women' (p. 73). But of course, today's students 'were not even born until after the critical years that link Anna Wulf with those of us who came of age, either chronologically or politically, about the time Lessing's novel was published'. Because they 'assume that all of the issues of social and gender equality have been adequately solved', most of Rubenstein's students 'tended to see Lessing's novel as "dated", Anna Wulf's problems as part of past history' (p. 73).

But Lessing herself admonishes us to 'remember that the book which bores you when you are twenty or thirty will open doors for you when you are forty or fifty' (1973, p. xviii). Some of the twenty-year-old women in Rubenstein's class may have been bored by *The Golden Notebook*, but they were told – because it was on the syllabus – that it was an 'important' book. Its prophetic urgency exists, *in potentia*, in their (sub)conscious, from which it may emerge, when they are forty or fifty, to open doors. And *The Golden*

Notebook is ticking like a time bomb on college syllabi all over the USA because Lessing scholars have persuaded their academic colleagues that she is a 'serious' writer. Paradoxically, it may be the professors who – in the long run – will keep Lessing 'alive and potent and fructifying and able to promote thought and discussion' (Lessing, 1973, p. xxii).

Doris Lessing loves paradox and champions ambiguity. If I were asked to write her epitaph, I'd unhesitatingly choose a sentence first articulated by Charles Watkins in her *Briefing for a Descent into Hell* and repeated in numerous interviews by Lessing: 'It isn't either or at all, it's and, and, and, and, and, and' (Lessing, 1971, p. 165). Therefore, although she despises academic criticism and has repeatedly denied that she writes as a feminist, I think she must be amused that in so far as there is an 'American' Lessing – as contradistinguished from a 'French' or 'South African' or 'Spanish' Lessing – she has been constructed and claimed by academic feminists who have proved themselves, over the last twenty years, to be maddeningly oxymoronic. They have not, to paraphrase Charles Watkins, privileged either 'the authority of experience' or the authority of Derrida, content or form, politics or academic isolationism. Collectively, they have been both empiricists and post-structuralists, grassroots activists and professional scholars. Perhaps, despite Lessing's disdain for them, they have – of all her readers – come the closest to comprehending the multifaceted genius of this protean author.

Notes

1. At the 1970 MLA Convention, Elaine Showalter poignantly outlined the plight of the female undergraduate English major, studying a canon which presented the story of Oedipus as *the* human tragedy because, 'as a professor remarked in a recent issue of *College English*, all of us want to kill our fathers and marry our mothers' (1971, p. 855).
2. At the time I wrote this essay, the 1987 MLA Bibliography was not yet available, so my figures for 1987 are incomplete.
3. And sales figures in themselves would not tell us much about Lessing's 'popular appeal'. As Terry Lovell has pointed out, academic appropriation of a book may actually boost sales. Indeed, 'sales may reach astronomical proportions as texts gain a secure place on the syllabus and become required reading for successive generations of students'. What Lovell says of Sillitoe's *Loneliness of the Long Distance Runner* and Golding's *Lord of the Flies* may be equally true of *The Golden Notebook*. These books 'owe their sales as much to their being taken up as school

texts as to their ability to entertain. . . . Objects of entertainment at the moment of their production, these works have survived by becoming primarily objects of study. Their sales today do not depend on their capacity still to please. Their market is guaranteed simply by their inclusion on the syllabus' (Lovell, pp. 135–6).

4. See, for example, Brooks, Cohen, Libby, Marchino, Markow, Morgan, Rapping and Spencer.

5. For a useful historical summary of feminist criticism, see Moi.

6. Patrocinio P. Schweickart invokes Saussure and Derrida; Gayle Greene enlists Barthes; in 1983, Betsy Draine used Barthes's notion of a 'braid of codes' to discuss Lessing's apparently conflicting use of the tropes of science fiction and of sacred literature in *Shikasta*; see Draine, pp. 143–86.

7. In July 1988, the Houston Grand Opera premiered *The Making of the Representative for Planet 8*, an opera by Philip Glass, with libretto by Doris Lessing, based on her 1982 novel, the fourth of the *Canopus in Argos* series. For an account of teaching *The Golden Notebook* in the context of such post-modernists as Vladimir Nobokov, Jorge Luis Borges, Thomas Pynchon, John Barth and Robert Coover, see Molly Hite, *'The Golden Notebook* in a Graduate Seminar'.

Works Cited

Allen, Walter. *The Modern Novel in Britain and the United States*. New York: E. P. Dutton, 1964.

Bergonzi, Bernard. *The Situation of the Novel*. Pittsburgh: University of Pittsburgh Press, 1970.

Brewster, Dorothy. *Doris Lessing*. New York: Twayne, 1965.

Brooks, Ellen W. 'The Image of Women in Lessing's *The Golden Notebook*'. *Critique* 15 (1973) 101–10.

Buckler, Ernest. Review of *The Golden Notebook*, by Doris Lessing. *New York Times Book Review* 1 July 1962: 4.

Burkom, Selma. 'Only Connect: Form and Content in the Works of Doris Lessing'. *Critique* 11 (1968): 315–45.

Carey, John L. 'Art and Reality in *The Golden Notebook*'. *Contemporary Literature* 14 (1973): 437–56.

Christ, Carol. *Diving Deep and Surfacing*. Boston, Mass: Beacon Press, 1980.

Cohen, Mary. 'Out of the Chaos, a New Kind of Strength: Doris Lessing's *The Golden Notebook*'. *The Authority of Experience*. Ed. Arlyn Diamond and Lee R. Edwards. Amherst: University of Massachusetts Press, 1977. 160–78.

Drabble, Margaret. 'Doris Lessing: Cassandra in a World Under Siege'. *Ramparts* February 1972: 50–4. Reprinted in Claire Sprague and Virginia Tiger, eds. *Critical Essays on Doris Lessing*. Boston: G. K. Hall, 1986. 183–91.

Draine, Betsy. *Substance under Pressure: Artistic Coherence and Evolving Form in the Novels of Doris Lessing*. Madison: University of Wisconsin Press, 1983.

Du Plessis, Rachel Blau. *Writing Beyond the Ending*. Bloomington: Indiana University Press, 1985.

Edwards, Lee R. *Psyche as Hero*. Middleton, Conn.: Wesleyan University Press, 1984.

Elshtain, Jean Bethke. 'The Post-*Golden Notebook* Fiction of Doris Lessing'. *Salamagundi* 47–8 (1980): 95–114.

Fitzgerald, E. J. Review of *This Was the Old Chief's Country*, by Doris Lessing. *Saturday Review* 2 August 1952: 19.

Franklin, H. Bruce. 'English as an Institution: The Role of Class'. *English Literature: Opening Up the Canon*. Selected Papers from the English Institute, 1979, n.s. 4. Ed. Leslie A. Fiedler and Houston A. Baker, Jr. Baltimore: The Johns Hopkins University Press, 1981. 92–106.

Greene, Gayle, 'Doris Lessing's *Landlocked*: "A New Kind of Knowledge"'. *Contemporary Literature* 28 (1987): 82–103.

Guillory, John. 'Canonical and Non-Canonical: A Critique of the Current Debate'. *ELH* 54 (1987): 483–527.

Review of *The Habit of Loving*, by Doris Lessing. *Time* 14 July 1958: 88.

Hite, Molly. '*The Golden Notebook* in a Graduate Seminar on Contemporary Experimental Fiction'. *Approaches to Teaching Lessing's 'Golden Notebook'*. Ed. Carey Kaplan and Ellen Cronan Rose. New York: MLA, 1989. 84–9.

Howe, Florence. 'A Conversation with Doris Lessing (1966)'. *Contemporary Literature* 14 (1973): 418–36.

Howe, Irving. '"Neither Compromise nor Happiness"'. Review of *The Golden Notebook*, by Doris Lessing'. *The New Republic* 15 December 1962: 17–20. Reprinted in Claire Sprague and Virginia Tiger, eds. *Critical Essays on Doris Lessing*. Boston: G. K. Hall, 1986. 177–8.

Hynes, Joseph. 'The Construction of *The Golden Notebook*'. *Iowa Review* 4.3 (1973): 100–13.

Kampf, Louis and Paul Lauter, eds. *The Politics of Literature: Dissenting Essays on the Teaching of English*. New York: Pantheon, 1972.

Kaplan, Carey and Ellen Cronan Rose, eds. *Doris Lessing: The Alchemy of Survival*. Athens, OH: Ohio University Press, 1988.

——. *Approaches to Teaching Lessing's* Golden Notebook. New York: MLA, 1989.

Kaplan, Sidney Janet. *Feminine Consciousness in the Modern British Novel*. Urbana: University of Illinois Press, 1975.

Karl, Frederick. *A Reader's Guide to the Contemporary English Novel*. New York: Farrar, Strauss and Giroux, 1963.

Karl, Frederick R. 'Doris Lessing in the Sixties: The New Anatomy of Melancholy'. *Contemporary Literature* 13 (1972): 15–33.

——. 'The Four-Gaited Beast of the Apocalypse: Doris Lessing's *The Four-Gated City*'. *Old Lines, New Forces*. Ed. Robert K. Morris. Cranbury, NJ: Associated Universities Press, 1976. 181–200.

Knapp, Mona. '*The Golden Notebook*: A Feminist Context for the Classroom'. *Approaches to Teaching Lessing's 'Golden Notebook'*. Ed. Carey Kaplan and Ellen Cronan Rose. New York: MLA, 1989. 108–14.

Leonard, John. 'The Spacing Out of Doris Lessing'. *New York Times Book Review* 7 February 1982: 1ff. Reprinted in Claire Sprague and Virginia

Tiger, eds. *Critical Essays on Doris Lessing*. Boston: G. K. Hall, 1986. 204–9.

Lessing, Doris. *Briefing for a Descent into Hell*. New York: Knopf, 1971.

——. *The Golden Notebook*. 1962. New York: Bantam, 1973.

'Lessing Society at MLA'. *Doris Lessing Newsletter* 3.2 (1979): 1.

Libby, Marion Vlastos. 'Sex and the New Woman in *The Golden Notebook*'. *Iowa Review* 5 (1974): 56–66.

Lovell, Terry. *Consuming Fiction*. London: Verso, 1987.

Magie, Michael L. 'Doris Lessing and Romanticism'. *College English* 38 (1977): 531–52.

Marchino, Lois. 'The Search for Self in the Novels of Doris Lessing'. *Studies in the Novel* 4 (1972): 252–62.

Markow, Alice Bradley. 'The Pathology of Feminine Failure in the Fiction of Doris Lessing'. *Critique* 16 (1975): 88–100.

McDowell, Frederick P. W. 'The Fiction of Doris Lessing: An Interim View'. *Arizona Quarterly* 21 (1965): 315–45.

Moi, Toril. *Sexual/Textual Politics: Feminist Literary Theory*. London: Methuen, 1985.

Morgan, Ellen. 'Alienation of the Woman Writer in *The Golden Notebook*'. *Contemporary Literature* 14 (1973): 471–80.

Peden, William. Review of *This Was the Old Chief's Country*, by Doris Lessing. *New York Times* 13 July 1952: 16.

——. Review of *The Habit of Loving*, by Doris Lessing. *New York Times* 20 July 1958: 4.

Porter, Nancy. 'Silenced History – *Children of Violence* and *The Golden Notebook*'. *World Literature Written in English* 12 (1973): 161–79.

Pratt, Annis. 'Introduction'. Special Number on Doris Lessing. *Contemporary Literature* 14 (1973): 413–17.

Rapping, Elayne Antler. 'Unfree Women: Feminism in Doris Lessing's Novels'. *Women's Studies* 3 (1975): 29–44.

Rigney, Barbara. *Madness and Sexual Politics in the Feminist Novel*. Madison: University of Wisconsin Press, 1978.

Rubenstein, Roberta. '*The Golden Notebook* in an Introductory Women's Studies Course'. *Approaches to Teaching Lessing's 'Golden Notebook'*. Ed. Carey Kaplan and Ellen Cronan Rose. New York: MLA, 1989. 72–7.

Schweickart, Patrocinio P. 'Reading a Wordless Statement: The Structure of Doris Lessing's *The Golden Notebook*'. *Modern Fiction Studies* 31 (1985): 263–79.

Seligman, Dee. 'Statement of Purpose'. *Doris Lessing Newsletter* 1.1 (1976): 2.

Showalter, Elaine. 'Women and the Literary Curriculum'. *College English* 32 (1971): 855–62.

——. *A Literature of Their Own: British Women Novelists from Brontë to Lessing*. Princeton: Princeton University Press, 1977.

——. 'Women's Time, Women's Space: Writing the History of Feminist Criticism'. *Feminist Issues in Literary Scholarship*. Ed. Shari Benstock. Bloomington: Indiana University Press, 1987. 30–44.

Spacks, Patricia Meyer. *The Female Imagination*. New York: Avon, 1975.

Spencer, Sharon. 'Femininity and the Woman Writer: Doris Lessing's *The*

Golden Notebook and the *Diary* of Anais Nin'. *Women's Studies* 1 (1973): 347–59.

Spilka, Mark. 'Lessing and Lawrence: The Battle of the Sexes'. *Contemporary Literature* 15 (1975): 218–40.

Sprague, Claire and Virginia Tiger, eds. *Critical Essays on Doris Lessing*. Boston: G. K. Hall, 1986.

Webb, Marilyn. 'Becoming the Men We Wanted to Marry'. *Village Voice* 4 January 1973: 1ff.

5

Cultures of Occupation and the Canadian [Con]Script[ion]: 'Lessing Changed My Life'

VIRGINIA TIGER

> **Maclean's:** *How would you like future generations to see Doris Lessing?*
>
> **Lessing:** I would like to be regarded as part of the civilizing influence and against fanaticism and the great mass orthodoxies, both secular and religious.   (Lurie, p. 8a)

Like loon to wintry wind-song, Canada warming to the cool, detached Doris Lessing of the later fiction should come as no paradox. *Shikasta, The Making of the Representative for Planet 8, The Good Terrorist, The Fifth Child*: these texts are cautionary; they challenge political extremisms, championing steadiness, judiciousness, individual independence, moderate iconoclasm in the face of ideologies. *Prisons We Choose to Live Inside* (1987) – a template exemplar of this voice with its (cranky) elucidations of psychological, sociological, anthropological and sociobiological contributions to a twentieth-century science of group behaviour – was, in fact, the published compendium of a lecture series dedicated to the late Right Honorable Vincent Massey, Governor General of Canada, who intended these Massey Lectures to be an international venue for the addressing of Western society's estate. (Lessing was to join a distinguished line of speakers: Northrop Frye, 1964; Martin Luther King, Jr, 1968; Claude Lévi-Strauss, 1978; Robert Jay Lifton, 1982; Carlos Fuentes, 1984.) As customary since 1961, the Canadian Broadcasting Corporation broadcast Lessing's lectures, their subtext – that we inhabit only the edge-tide of civilisation – striking familiar chords in a country forced by climate as much as geography and history to become expert at national compromise, international mediation: sighting powerful opponents and disarming their volatilities by sheer resoluteness.

Thus Canada's preference for the later Lessing.[1] Rooted in wary scepticism – as tenaciously as moss to rock mulch – Lessing's idiosyncratic (some would say, neo-conservative) attitudes, now so full-blossomed, are strategies for survival an observer early on, and more frequently than supposed, forges. So Lessing's stance is no stranger to English Canada whose literature, littered throughout the nineteenth century by the corpses of more than crass casualty, shows the country's abiding sense of seige. Having played for over two centuries a permanent double game, Canada approaches, for example, international affairs quietly, moderately, multilaterally.

A collection of colonies under rivalling French and English rule from the seventeenth century until Confederation in 1867, Canada's sensibility (even in French Quebec) was dominated well into this century by British texts, teachers and everywhere British talismans. An illustration: my sharpest recollection of experiencing Canada as what I now would term a British cultural colony; I am standing to sing 'God Save Our Gracious Queen' (the then preferred National Anthem) before a picture – as ubiquitously displayed on cinema screens as classroom walls – of a scarlet uniformed Queen Elizabeth, astride a horse intently reviewing her regiment while the Union Jack floats imperiously overhead. Independent from England though the country was, one stood to attention out of obligatory respect for empire.

But the nation Canada had reasons more taxing than ritual for standing erect, that being the least vulnerable posture when gazing southward. For there lay the other imperialism, all the more monolithic for its glamour; like the well-behaved schoolchild, one folded one's hands and stared solemnly. Suspiciously, often longingly. Queen Elizabeth's cameo appearance on those screens might provoke a passing acknowledgement, but the real point about the screens was that they showed movies, all of which were American: like the comic books, the magazines, the novels one read as well as the sociology, the political science, the philosophy, the economy. The latter, of course, was the childishly simple reason for Canada's cultural indenture to America, the Canadian government in the postwar decade having permitted the sale of natural resources to the Uncle Sam of the extended hand. To this day, I remember an inchoate grief on hearing from my father that his company (Canadian Oil, then the last remaining Canadian-owned concern in a country unctuous with crude oil) had that morning become an American subsidiary. So, of course, with ten times the Canadian population and more or less ten times the riches, the United States never needed to find puzzling the status of Canada as an extension of its political and economic spheres. Canadians (me included) piloted their independence delicately, of course, reassuring the States of amity, on the one hand, while resisting its none too avuncular influence on the other.

The Canadian reception of Doris Lessing then is intimately tied to the country's cultural schizophrenia as simultaneously a British and American colony. The works it has chosen to embrace since the 1960s reflect its slow weaning away from colonialism and its emergence in the 1970s into the confident years of nationalism, years symbolised by Pierre Elliott Trudeau, the prime minister who proposed the middle broker role for Canada and in himself presented 'a new model Canadian: half-French, half-English, a world traveller, a sophisticate, a snob, an intellectual' (Cohen 4).

Fittingly, the first Canadian response to Lessing was to review the very book most neglected in the United States (Walker, p. 14). Appearing in 1960 in Toronto's *Globe and Mail*, the newspaper whose literary opinion has always been most widely respected, was an appreciation of *In Pursuit of the English*, the book title evoking for Canadians precisely the quest undertaken in those years by every aspiring Canadian novelist who, like Mordecai Richler, felt compelled to flee the provincial backwater for England. The social and working-class reportorial themes of *In Pursuit* clearly appealed to Canadian reviewers, who made frequent references to other social diagnosticians, all British. Lessing was compared to George Eliot (like her predecessor, 'she continually chooses the big canvas'; Engel, p. 35); to D. H. Lawrence (like his, her short stories 'compassionately render the malaise of class and divided loyalties'; Carroll, p. 29); E. M. Forster ('[a]s in his work, the sense of life's essential cruelty is mitigated by an absorption in personal relations'; Duffy, p. 19); Charles Dickens ('*In Pursuit*'s author, unlike most contemporary middle-class English writers, has the vitality of Shakespeare and Dickens; this book might well be called "Room at the Bottom"' Goldsborough, p. 102) Clearly Lessing was being read in the context of the complex Canadian sense of displacement from and reverence for things English. No trace of a review of *The Golden Notebook* can be found in 1962, the year of its English and

American publication.[2] Indeed, compared to the plentiful number of critical studies in the USA, only a cursory exposition of its depiction of 'female heroism' (Joanne Craig's '*The Golden Notebook*: The Novelist as Heroine') appeared the year after its paperback reissue in 1973. And although as early as 1964, Lessing is being introduced in the Canadian equivalent of the *New York Times Book Review* as a significant woman writer, (author of *The Golden Notebook*), the University of Toronto professor reviewing *A Man and Two Women* foregrounded the déraciné, exilic qualities of her imagination: 'A former Southern African now living in England, Mrs Lessing is at her best when dramatising individuals lost between the lines of class or cut off from their roots . . . Caught in these situations, her characters engage in comic, grotesque, or tragic attempts to make contact, to place themselves socially and spiritually' (Carroll, p. 29).

The sense of being overshadowed, so much a staple of the Canadian sensibility, found then its welcoming literary correspondence in the Lessing texts most scarred by the mental condition emerging from a colonial past. It is not the zealot of *A Ripple from the Storm* but the exiled Martha Quest of *The Four-Gated City* who commands comment, one reviewer describing, as though it were a paradigmatic United Nations address from a Canadian ambassador, the novel's concerns with 'public, governmental and ultimately international stupidities which have led to erosions of liberty, the pollution of air, earth and water and the proliferation of nuclear and chemical weapons' (Buithenhuis, p. 16).

The year 1973 marks a critical turning-point in the assessment of Doris Lessing, her work now situated in a climate charged by the intellectual exuberance of two heady currents of change: cultural nationalism and the new feminism. Out of an explosion of literary talent in the sixties and seventies, an explosion not unconnected with a general increase in national consciousness and confidence at the time, emerged a new Canadian literature roughly dating from the appearance of Margaret Laurence's *The Stone Angel* (1964). Critics, writers, editors and broadcasters,[3] among them Northrop Frye, Mavis Gallant, Robert Weaver, Robin Mathews, Robert Fulford and Margaret Atwood, regularly discussed Canada's 'identity crisis'. Indeed, Atwood's *Survival*, a thematic guide to Canadian literature, was written under the 'outraged surprise' that 'my country's literature was not just British literature imported or American literature with something missing' (Atwood, p. 237).

Anglophone writers like Marian Engel, Matt Cohen, Audrey Thomas and Leonard Cohen found a greedy audience, intoxicated by national pride and hungry for things Canadian. An artistic infrastructure, which included the Canadian Broadcasting Corporation, the Canada Council for the Arts, the Literary Press Group and the Union Nationale des Ecrivains, generously supported authors, artists, film-makers and little magazines. Aided by such sponsorship, a fall in the price of paper and changes in printing technology, small presses started up in Toronto, Winnipeg, Edmonton and Vancouver providing publication sources for writers, many of whom having earlier been told by the foreign-controlled industry that novels were publishable only when co-publication in New York or London was found. If Canadian writers such as Atwood, Laurence, Richler, Alice Munro, Robertson Davies or Farley Mowat have found international readership in the last two decades that appreciation was won in part because a cultural nationalism transformed the way Canada read – and therefore wrote – itself. For as the poet F. R. Scott predicted in the twenties: 'What will be written in the full culture of occupation / Will come presently, tomorrow / From millions whose hands can turn these rocks into children' (p. 97).

Scott's creation metaphor aside, nationality and gender are not necessarily good bedfellows, their cravings being at bottom too similar: the need to have difference annotated. I have described the Canadian literary renaissance in order to explain why Lessing's work was presented in the seventies through the lens of feminism. The overlap between creative writing and academic criticism, which is a striking feature of Canadian letters (like Clark Blaise and Barry Callaghan, most writers do not specialise in one genre and many are professors) meant that critical theories and taxonomies were developed by and tested on Canadian writers, as an analysis of the influential scholarly journal *Canadian Literature* would certainly indicate.

It is not until *Shikasta*'s publication in 1979 that the conflation of literary texts and archetypally informed critical paradigms can be detected: by then Lessing's first and final preoccupation, survival, was being read through a Canadian sensibility, itself early formed by just such a theme. Woman-centred readings of *Memoirs of a Survivor*, for example, Lorelei Cederstrom's article in *Mosaic*, a useful absorption of Frye's categories as they relate to survival narratives, opened channels. (Indeed, her conclusion about the vexatious conclusion of the *Memoirs* is, by way of its thematic play with displacement, survival and recreation, coloured by characteristically Canadian hues. The narrator 'is a Survivor of the experience; she remembers it and lives to tell about it so that others can share the experience. As a "Survivor," she has established a new relationship to the world. . . . She has moved from the world in which she was not the master of her own house. . . . Ultimately, she has achieved individuation . . . vitalised by links with a living symbolic heritage'; Cederstrom, p. 130.) By the time male critics, reviewers and readers had become drawn to Lessing's otherworldly landscapes, a feminist critique of her work had completed the ground-tilling whose ironic growth was the privileging once again of androcentric readings: 'Has this master of realism, this prophet of feminism turned to writing *Star Wars*, for intellectuals', wondered *Maclean's* (Abley, 1979, p. 62), voicing a belief that the texts would no longer threaten by their subversion of male symbolic systems. (In this context, though digressively, one can not but speculate that Lessing's strenuous *apologiae* for the *Canopus* series were not entirely unconnected to the male readership she regained.)

In an earlier analysis of Lessing's critical reception, Claire Sprague and I observed that its acuity might well be accounted for by the striking fact that many of her reviewers (Joyce Carol Oates, Joan Didion, Gore Vidal, Rebecca West, Kingsley Amis, Margaret Drabble) were novelists themselves, 'able to scissor through an established reputation and meet Lessing's strengths and weaknesses head-on'.[4] Unquestionably, Lessing's reputation in English Canada gained ascendancy in the seventies because her books were reviewed – and rigorously so – in the *Globe and Mail* by two of Canada's most distinguished women novelists: Marian Engel and Margaret Laurence. With her African novel, *This Side Jordan*, and collection of African stories based on her experience in Somalia and Ghana as well as her series of Manawaka novels – *The Stone Angel, A Jest of the Gods, The Fire-Dwellers, The Diviners* – Laurence could well be considered the Canadian equivalent of Doris Lessing. Thus Laurence's review of *Memoirs of a Survivor* is all the more illuminating for its introductory paragraph, coming from a writer familiar with the situation of the Canadian publishing industry and the ways in which writers, trapped by – as Lessing would put it – 'a cage of associations', can only be released into informed readings when a body of work is viewed in its totality. Laurence writes:

First a compliment and a complaint. Full marks to General Publishing for having obtained the Canadian rights to Doris Lessing's new novel. But why did they not include a list of her other books and a brief biographical note? We can assume that most readers are familiar with Lessing's work, but still, one forgets in which year any particular novel or book of stories was published; one can't quite remember when it was that Doris Lessing left South Africa and went to England. (Laurence, p. 36)

As equally significant as the emphasis on cultural exile here is the implication – present by absence – that women novelists (even those of Margaret Laurence's stature) must place their own work in the context of Lessing's achievement. For the generation of women writers who came of age during the 1970s, Lessing's work carried a deeply felt, and often influential, impact.

Thus Marian Engel's observation (in her review of *The Summer Before the Dark*) that Lessing 'keeps on turning the ball of reality to the mirror of the mind, recording the glancing light always at a different angle' (Engel, p. 35) is as much a comment on Engel's practice (in, for example, her controversial novel, *Bear*) as an admiration of the realistic strategy in Lessing's project; 'When she tackles real dilemmas she is fascinating and when she is Doris Lessing she is unbeatable'. Engel comments elsewhere (Engel, 1979, p. 9), summarising a specifically female and characteristically Canadian view of the author at this time. Her texts instructed others by their unhurried rendering of quotidian matters (dress, decor, food), the simple naming and describing of observed realities being the enterprise most gripping to writers overcoming cultural colonialism – women writers overcoming 'the status of being a colony . . . within the Canadian colony' (Sullivan p. x).

As to Lessing's popular appeal in Canada – it being now all but axiomatic that women readers experience gendered identification with her female characters whether mirrorings occur in Japan, Argentina or Israel – it was once again an informal community of women which nurtured initial affections. To the scents of memory I here incline, recalling how I came to read her work. It was my first Thanksgiving leagues from my parents' dining-room and neither festivity nor month seemed at all Canadian, both being heraldically American. Our hostess, a faculty wife, asked me to help in the kitchen; I was incredulous, so sacerdotally did I cherish my calling as a graduate student that I assumed it automatically released one from domestic chores. While off-handedly spooning to an entrée dish sweet potatoes (yams she called them, I noted testily), she told me that her favourite novelist was Doris Lessing. That she was reading *Children of Violence* and that I might borrow it after she'd had the baby.

Baby! Books! I was horrified and vowed, that day of pool-clear youth, never to have babies, never to be over twenty-two and plump, and never ever to chat about women's novels next to steaming stoves.

Of course, I was a good girl – well-bred, as maiden aunts murmured over cups of English tea – and went to visit this disheartening person who'd done the quite irrevocable act of parturition. The baby was brought by probably and, of it, I have no recollection. What I remember – and it sits still on shelves above my desk – was the thick, grey volume given me: the binding read:

Doris Lessing
CHILDREN OF VIOLENCE
Martha Quest
A
Proper Marriage
SIMON AND
SCHUSTER

Of course, it changed my life, a phrase I have since heard in dozens of places: at diplomatic parties on New York's East Side, over barley-wines in Knightsbridge pubs, while eating blood-sausages at asados in Buenos Aires. Everywhere, ordinary women readers were captivated by a writer who honoured, indeed re-claimed, women's experience, and – like me, at that time – nudged close to a voice, though they possessed no critical vocabulary to describe its valences.

It is not then surprising – or even Canadian – that from 1973 until *Shikasta*'s publication Lessing was seen very much as a woman writing for other women; only women reviewed her books, appraisals appearing in publications as various as *Chatelaine*, a mainstream (and progressive) 'women's magazine' (Anderson, p. 6), *Priorities*, a house-organ for the Women's Caucus of the New Democratic Party, Canada's Socialist party (Yandle, pp. 26–8), *The Canadian Forum*, a prestigious journal of opinion on the arts and politics (McCallum, pp. 56–7), *Queen's Quarterly*, Queen's University' academic journal (McSweeney, 1973, pp. 666–9), and the feminist literary forum, *A Room of One's Own* (McSweeney, 1979, pp. 46–53).

Reiterative as Lessing's disavowals of contemporary feminism continue to be,[5] feminocentric critics in Canada (as elsewhere) have claimed her, happily or hauntingly, as their own. Academicians, for the most part, used Lessing's works as a means to elucidate issues and problems relevant to women in patriarchy (Flood; McCauley). Even when textual sublations of narratological forms were critiqued (as in Pamela McCallum's analysis in the *Canadian Forum* of historicised autobiography in *Memoirs* or my tracing of *The Golden Notebook*'s modification of the eighteenth-century confessional mode [Tiger, pp. 472–87]) authorial authority was never decentred. Conspicuous too by absence were readings juxtaposing Canadian novels on the question of womanhood with comparable Lessing texts. My hunch is that Lessing was read during this period as displaced from the intense, exhausting debate on Canadian culture, fuel for which I find in the fact that the première danseuse of CanLit Letters, Margaret Atwood (whose provocative *Survival* prompted sheets of magazine commentary the very year that Lessing's *Summer Before the Dark* was being acclaimed elsewhere by Atwood's peers, Erica Jong and Margaret Drabble) never once reviewed a Lessing book. Sweet-suited lovers nationalism and feminism seldom are.

'The central symbol for Canada . . . is undoubtedly Survival, *la Survivance*. . . . A preoccupation with one's survival is necessarily also a preoccupation with the obstacles to that survival', Atwood's *Survival* observed (1972, p. 33), all but presciently sighting the third phase of the Doris Lessing reception in Canada. Whereas exilic colonialism attracted in the first years and woman-centred exegeses followed, it was the (elsewhere dismissed) series, *Canopus in Argos*, which fed Canadian mythologies, its rock-hard and wind-blown otherworldly perspective matching the Canadian archetypal experience of seige. So, for example, quite the most synoptic review of *Shikasta* – by Michael Thorpe, a Lessing scholar – appeared in the *Canadian Forum*:

> Like Johor in the novel, Lessing sees our Earth as in its Last Days, closing a Century of Destruction; her mission . . . is to alert a saving remnant who will ensure the continuity and

regeneration of life after the apocalypse. The latter part of *Shikasta*
enlarges upon and refines the brief Appendix to *The Four-Gated
City*. It completes the relinquishment of her ideal urban vision
which seemingly had its last death with the disintegrating
London of *Memoirs of a Survivor*, and points in Old Testament
fashion the way back to renewal in the desert places.   (Thorpe,
p. 34)

Finally, the *Canopus in Argos* series drew a far more considerate
and generous reception in Canadian newspapers, magazines and
scholarly journals than in other countries.[6] The fables seemed – in
one commentator's felicitous phrase – 'requiems for ourselves'
(Abley, 1983, p. 57). *The Making of the Representative for Planet 8*,
with its construction of a giant wall around a freezing, dying
planet, proved especially evocative, stirring – I suspect – the fitful
fatalism deep in the soul of a people made tractable by climate, land
mass, with that legacy's injunction to forge communal resources for
survival. *Making* matches other matters quintessentially Canadian,
its elegiac sternness (no more oxymoronic an atmosphere than its
felix theme that fall is fortunate) sharing a tone Northrop Frye in
The Bush Garden observes having located:

I have long been impressed in Canadian poetry by a tone of
deep terror in regard to nature. . . . It is not a terror of the
dangers or discomforts or even the mysteries of nature, but a
terror of the soul at something that these things manifest.   (Frye,
p. 78)

'For my father, who used to sit, hour after hour, night after
night, outside our house in Africa, watching the stars. "Well," he
would say, "if we blow ourselves up, there's plenty more where
we came from!"' reads the epigraph to Re: Colonised Planet 5
Shikasta. The informing authorial code here neatly pinpoints the
Canadian reception of Doris Lessing. Like Africa, Canada strands
individuals in vast territories, for one the dry-stinging then swollen
veld, for the other the swampy then ice-sharded bush. Above, a
dome addresses the unimportance of the human, merely another
participant in the chaos of matter. When writers make any sense
of this [dis]placement, they chart territories, that 'map-making . . .
the discovery of where things are in relation to each other' being –
as Margaret Atwood so astutely remarks in a memory-essay on

Northrop Frye – a distinctive feature of the Canadian habit of mind (Atwood, 1984, p. 405). Thus the Canadian figure (named rather inelegantly 'the megasystem thinker') chooses – like Frye or Marshall McLuhan – interconnecting spatial metaphors, while British critics impose social classifications and Americans tear structural wholes, impose isolate parts, invent systemic taxonomies. In such a context, Lessing's work is, of course, implacably that of the map-maker. And Canada has come to cherish the connective artisan, one who names – the 'naming-game', remember, appeared early on with Anna's strategy for mounting anxieties by imagining first a room, an apartment, a street, a borough, a city, a country: another country – and charts new worlds and old.

Acknowledgements

The research for this article was supported by a grant from the Rutgers University Graduate School at Newark. I am especially grateful to Dean Donald G. Stein. To Julia Creet, my research assistant from the graduate program at the Ontario Institute for Studies in Education, I tip my hat, her search and seize skills being splendid.

Notes   *244450*

1. Interviewed in 1986 by *Maclean's*, in an article (rather righteously) titled 'Fighting Fanaticism', Lessing discussed what was then her most recent novel, *The Good Terrorist*, whose apparent disavowal of political dissidence had provoked distress internationally. Canada, historically discomfited by political extremism, acclaimed the work, accepting uncritically Lessing's account that she 'wasn't making a political statement about youth or the whole of the left: the book is about a certain kind of person in Europe, one who was also common in North America in the 1970s' (Lurie, p. 8a).
2. A complete bibliography of the Canadian reception of Doris Lessing was compiled, the following search tools being used: *Book Review Digest; Canadian Magazine Index; Canadian Newspaper Index; Canadian Periodicals Index; Combined Retrospective Index to Book Reviews in Scholarly Journals; Current Book Review Citations; Index to Book Reviews in the Humanities*. For the feminist reception, indexes to the following journals were consulted: *A Room of One's Own; Atlantis; Branching Out; Broadside; Canadian Women's Studies; Fireweed; Resources for Feminist Research*.
3. In Canada there is a vast overlap between creative writing, academic criticism and broadcasting (both on radio and television), the CBC – like the BBC – being a public institution. Short stories, for example, have been read on radio since 1938 when Robert Weaver started a weekly programme on Canadian writers.

4. Sprague and Tiger, p. 22. We also made the point that the 'criticism reflected in these reviews in no way corresponds to Lessing's generally dismissive attitude to what she considers the parasitic role of reviewers'.

5. To what *Quill and Quire* described as 'a crowd of 500 adoring Doris Lessing fans [who] packed the Brigantine Room at Toronto's Habourfront on March 27 1984'. Lessing remarked categorically that the women's movement 'has been very disappointing to me from the start. I think it has vanished in a great sea of talk. . . . A law being changed does more than a thousand complaints about how nasty one's father was when you were 10' (*Quill and Quire* 50 (May 1984): 22).

6. *The Sirian Experiments* (which many regard as one of the least compelling volumes in the series) was nationally reviewed (and sometimes revered); for example (by Marian Engel) in *the Globe and Mail* (21 February 1981): 54–5; in *Chatelaine* 54 (April 1981): 12; in *Quill and Quire* (a trade journal for Canadian publications) 47 (July 1981): 66; the *Canadian Forum* 61: 710 (June–July 1981): 34–5; the *Montreal Gazette* (11 April 1981): 61; the *Vancouver Sun* (21 February 1981): L37; the *Toronto Star* (7 March 1981): F11.

Works Cited

Abley, Mark. 'In the Century of Destruction'. *Maclean's Magazine* 26 November 1979: 62, 64.
——'Joy in the Face of Extinction'. *Maclean's Magazine* 5 April 1983: 57–8.
Anderson, Doris. '*The Summer Before the Dark*'. *Chatelaine* September 1973: 6.
Atwood, Margaret. *Survival: A Thematic Guide to Canadian Literature*. Toronto: House of Anansi Press, 1972.
——'Northrop Frye Observed'. *Second Words: Selected Critical Prose*. Boston: Beacon Press, 1984. 389–414.
Buitenhuis, Peter. 'Spotlight on the Unseen Centre of Our Time'. *Globe and Mail Magazine* 12 July 1969: 16.
Carroll, John. '*A Man and Two Women*'. *Globe and Mail Magazine* 29 February 1964: 29.
Cederstrom, Lorelei. '"Inner Space" Landscape: Doris Lessing's *Memoirs of a Survivor*'. *Mosaic* 13.3–4 (1980): 115–32.
Cohen, Matt. 'Literary Nationalism in English Canada: Boqus or Magus'. *American Book Review* 10.2 (1988): 3–4.
Craig, Joanne. '*The Golden Notebook*: The Novelist as Heroine'. *University of Windsor Review* 10.1 (1974): 55–66.
Duffy, Denis. 'Sense, Morality and the Diary'. *Globe and Mail Magazine* 6 April 1985: 19.
Engel, Marian. 'It's Not How Women Ought to Live, Just How They Have to'. *Globe and Mail* [Toronto, Ont.] 12 May 1973: 35.
——'*Shikasta*'. *Globe and Mail* [Toronto, Ont.] 15 December 1979: 9.
Flood, Cynthia. 'Doris Lessing: Architect of the Soul'. *A Room of One's Own* 5.4 (1980): 26–34.
Frye, Northrop. *The Bush Garden*. Toronto: House of Anansi Press, 1971.

Goldsborough, Diana. *'In Pursuit of the English'*. *Tamarack Review* 19.4 (1961): 102.

Laurence, Margaret. 'Doris Lessing's Vision: A Chilling Apocalypse'. *Globe and Mail* [Toronto, Ont.] 7 June 1976: 36.

Lurie, Theodora. 'Fighting Fanticism'. *Maclean's* 10 February 1986: 8a, 8c.

McCallum, Pamela. 'Survival Gear'. *Canadian Forum* December 1974: 26–8.

McCauley, Carole. 'Doris Lessing: Shapes of Pain, Patterns of Recovery'. *Fireweed* 2.2 (1979): 8–18.

McSweeney, Kerry. 'Editorial'. *Queen's Quarterly* 80.3 1973: 666–9.

——. 'The Later Doris Lessing'. *A Room of One's Own* 4.3 (1979): 46–53.

Scott, F. R. 'Laurentian Shield'. *Poets Between the Wars*. Ed. Milton Wilson. Toronto: New Canadian Library, 1970. 97.

Sprague, Claire and Virginia Tiger. 'Introduction'. *Critical Essays on Doris Lessing*. Ed. Claire Sprague and Virginia Tiger. Boston: G. K. Hall, 1986. 1–26.

Sullivan, Rosemary. 'Introduction'. *Stories By Canadian Women*. Ed. Rosemary Sullivan. Toronto: Oxford University Press, 1984. i–xix.

Thorpe, Michael. 'Space Fiction'. *Canadian Forum* October 1980: 32.

Tiger, Virginia. 'The Female Novel of Education and the Confessional Heroine'. *Dalhousie Review* 60 (1980): 472–87.

Walker, Joan. *'In Pursuit of the English'*. *Globe and Mail* [Toronto, Ont.] 26 November 1960: 14.

Yandle, Sharon. 'Looking at Lessing'. *Priorities* 2.12 (1974): 26–8.

6

Doris through the French Looking-Glass

NICOLE WARD JOUVE

The (female) reviewer has read *The Golden Notebook*:

> Months pass, the story the book has told recedes . . ., But its
> flesh. Enormous, obese, deformed. And the heaviness in my
> hands, into which I rush, in which I swim, explore myself,
> search for myself, remain hidden, buried in the belly-book – and
> the desire, the nostalgia violently revived, oh initiating mother,
> mother found again, with whom the bond has been tied again,
> mother open to the world, to knowledge, the body of men, free
> mother, all-powerful mother perhaps, adventurous adventured
> mother, exposed, engrossed, mother mother always, show
> yourself to me, let me see how, where, to cross, from me to
> you.   (Clédat, p. 56)

This could only be France. And it could only be the 1970s. Only in
the place and at the time in which écriture féminine' was being
propounded by Hélène Cixous, the Editions des femmes and such
magazines as *Sorcières* where the above passage comes from could
such a review be written. *Le Carnet d'or* which burst upon the
French scene in 1976 owed much of the raving reception that it
got to the blossoming of the women's movement in that particular
period.

There is irony in this. For it was just the kind of welcome Lessing
herself did not want. She said that she had left all that stuff behind
twenty years before, she said that she felt that a 'dead baby' was
being brought back into the world. She reacted with cold fury to
feminist or 'écriture féminine' readings of *The Golden Notebook*. She
asked *Le Monde* interviewer Françoise Wagener what she saw in
Le Carnet d'or (God knows, the line of *Le Monde* was never pro-
feminist!). Françoise Wagener replied that she admired it because

it was 'a classic, a *summa*, a great introspective book, a descent
into the hell of the female ego, and an illustrating testimony on
the present age' (Wagener). A lesser person might have been
pleased. Wouldn't you, if somebody said that about one of your
books? And there was nothing 'feminist' about the reply. Lessing
tartly retorted that women were locking her up in a ghetto, and
that she'd like to be read by men as well. An unfair request, since
at least half the reviewers were men, and full of praise. *GN* won
the Prix Médicis Etranger, which is prestigious: it is mostly men
who sit on the jury. But that she should have chosen poor Wagener
for her outburst shows how much she wanted to dissociate herself
from the reading the women's movement was giving her.

Biting the hand that, after all, fed her, Lessing reminds me of
Goethe and Chateaubriand, who in their mature years barked at
the progeny of little Werthers and Renés which their novels had
spawned. Young men all over Europe were identifying with the
'mal du siècle' they had expressed and they, the great men who
had gone beyond it, almost loathed those who were now modelling
themselves on their early creations, or identifying with them.
Perhaps writers do not like readers to be mirrors to their own
mirror-images? Is it the reappropriation that bothers them? Do
they feel their souls, their doubles, are being stolen? Or that the
unique and the fictitious, Werther, René, Anna Wulf, are being
cheapened by becoming many, becoming real? Even though they,
the writers, all along, had wanted to express the mood of the age?

The passage from *Sorcières* which I started from may be over-
lyrical, loose, almost comically dated. Yet it strives for something
that would go beyond normal reviewing. Editors tend to expect
that reviews be a blend of précis and criticism, with some erudition
or plenty of verbal antics thrown in according to the style of the
journal. The reviewer must make it clear that s/he is here, sitting
with 'us' in judgement, and the book there, to be appraised or
praised. Re-view: to see again, to reflect, to turn the mirror upon
something and act as a relay to the many, the potential or
prospective readers. The eye, the distance in the eye, is of the
essence. Though it must be said that the metaphor, here as with
the famous mirror-image of realism, erases the act of construction,
the selectiveness, the distortions, the omissions, and above all the
ideological projection that the very existence of specific modes of
reviewing entails. But the writer from *Sorcières* is striving to express
a deeper experience of reading, the way a book can become part

of you, change your life. She is allowing Lessing to go through the looking-glass. She is right about *GN*, as is that other female reviewer from the Belgian *Cahiers du Grif* who marvels that a book written in and about the fifties should be so totally recognisable in the seventies. That does say something about the time-effect of Lessing's works. Though they were, up to *The Four-Gated City*, about the author's past, they always somehow anticipated the future. *Quest* was always in and of them, making reality bizarrely hollow – or peculiarly invalidating their own apparent realistic mode. They were certainly impatient of the present, as was Simone de Beauvoir, with whom several French reviewers compare Lessing. With de Beauvoir the quest was a 'project' towards something ahead. Lessing was seeking to transcend time. The mind-motion of her characters, and often that of her sentences, was in expanding centrifugal circles. They strove to reach the state where the eye of the hurricane goes still and turns liquid, where a Survivor goes through the wall or Al·Ith goes, not through the looking-glass, but all the same into the blue of Zone Two. Much of Lessing's work, you could argue, acts like the mediaeval *concave* mirror, a symbol of infinity.

The publishing of Lessing in France, and its timing, or rather mistiming, suggest the reverse image: that of a convex mirror. *Vaincue par la brousse* (a romantic and inappropriate title for *The Grass Is Singing*) was published by Plon in 1953. After that, not a single Lessing was translated until 1976, the date of *Le Carnet d'or*. That was a huge success. The publishers, Albin Michel who, they claimed, wanted to acquaint the public with the 'big', the 'great' Lessing first, followed in 1978, with perfect disregard of chronology, organic or formal unity, with three, not five, volumes of *The Children of Violence*. The first volume, incidentally, was dated 1964, not 1954, the two years that had elapsed between *La Carnet d'or* (1976) and *Les Enfants de la violence* (1978) being somehow converted into a false actual span, suggesting that Lessing had written *Martha Quest* and *A Proper Marriage* after *The Golden Notebook* (1962). I remember Jeanne Rollin-Weisz, the producer of the radio show 'Un livre, des voix' whom I helped on a programme on *Les Enfants de la violence* voicing her amazement that anybody *could* write *Martha Quest* after *Le Carnet d'or* . . .

Then Lessing flooded the market. The African storie₋ were out at the end of 1980, *La Cité promise* (*FGC*) early 1981, followed in the same year by *L'Eté avant la nuit* (*The Summer Before The Dark*),

Un Homme et deux femmes (*A Man and Two Women*) and *Shikasta* –
the *Canopus* series having been bought under a separate deal by
Le Seuil, which carried on publication of the later volumes in the
eighties. Meanwhile Albin Michel produced *Les Mémoires d'une
survivante* in 1982 and the two volumes of *Jane Somers* in 1985 and
1986. Those were published under Lessing's own name and
were a great success. They, together with *Les Chats en particulier*
(*Particularly Cats*), 1984, rate as numbers one and two of Lessing's
oeuvre according to a recent critic. *The Good Terrorist* came out at
the end of 1986 (*La Terroriste*).

Ten years of Lessing in France (1976–86) thus correspond to forty
years of Lessing's writing and publishing in her native language. I
say this reminds me of a convex mirror in that the French time-
span miniaturises and deforms the English publishing time, as
well as the time of writing, and also spatialises it. It is as if Lessing's
books had been there as objects to be arranged in whatever
commercial order suited the publishers. The new books (like the
Canopus series) were brought out side by side with those that had
been in existence a long time. Thus the lived dimension of Lessing's
work, writing as process and progress, the fact that she has always
written in a state of imaginary contemporaneity with herself, what
was bothering her at a particular moment of history and moment
of her own intellectual and emotional evolution, has been erased.
Some French reviewers noted this. 'Have pity on Lessing', 'Pitié
pour Lessing', is the title of one article (Rocher; see also Fogel).
You are publishing her in such disorder you are 'murdering' her,
another, Cathy Bernheim, accused, pointing out that to publish
Shikasta before either *Briefing* or *Memoirs* made it impossible for the
French readership to understand what Lessing was up to.

Other distortions occurred. Because *Le Carnet d'or* was published
first, it was somehow assumed it had been written first, even
though people often knew otherwise. Later publications elicit
comparisons with it, are regarded as falling off the mark, not
being up to the standard of the earlier work. It is regarded as
'quintessential'. One reviewer of *Les Enfants de la violence* (the first
two books) says that it is like a rough draft of *GN*, assuming that
Lessing knew all along she was going to write *GN* (Xénakis). *Jane
Somers* is described as 'one of the veins' running through *Le Carnet
d'or*. The connection was, to say the least, suggested to French
readers (and with how much justice?) by the translation into the
title *Les Carnets de Jane Somers*. Though there is *The Diary of a Good*

Neighbour, nowhere is there the use of the term '*notebook*'. No doubt for good reasons.

The title *The Golden Notebook* was taken literally. It became the measure of all else that Lessing had written and that subsequently came out in France, a kind of *gold* standard for the rest of her work. All that was known about Lessing herself, and there was much that was by 1976, was channelled by the publishers and used to construct Lessing the novelist as almost more important or of more concern than the novel that was currently coming out. France may be the country of Barthes and Co., of the attempt to replace the notion of The Author and His/Her Books with that of the Text. When it came to brass tacks, i.e. selling Lessing, the Author and Her Books shone in all their (golden) glory. The Author's life was used to inform the books. *GN* was read as autobiography, almost transparent autobiography, straightway. So were *the Children of Violence*, the African stories, *Memoirs, The Summer* – and *Jane Somers*! A unified and non-contradictory personality was on sale from the first, retrospective or prospective knowledge erasing the immediate impact and effect of surprise the books had when they came out in England or the USA, and the question of what autobiography actually is for Lessing, how it functions, never being properly asked.

Indeed, I have been wondering if Lessing didn't give such a surprisingly large number of interviews in France, especially in 1981, the year in which four of her books came out, because she was seeking to oppose the counterfeit vision that was being generated. She let herself be interviewed at least eight times for both press and television in 1981, five times in 1984–5: and she is supposed to be a lady whom it is difficult to interview! Perhaps she was just enjoying its being France, the strangeness, the foreignness. But she very much used the occasions. She protested against misinterpretations, pointed to lines of continuity, as between the end of *La Cité promise* and *Shikasta*. She insisted that Proust was one of her great models, no one having compared her to Proust, though 'Shakespeare, Goethe, Dante' were named by one interviewer[1] (oh the inflation of critical speech!), and she was compared to – hold your breath – Nadine Gordimer, André Brink, D. H. Lawrence, Joseph Conrad, Graham Greene, Charlotte Brontë, George Eliot, Joyce Carol Oates, Kate Millet, Mary McCarthy, Anais Nin, Jean Rhys . . . The rationale of the comparisons seems to lie in what English-language writers the reviewer has read, and especially has had to review. But reading those interviews, you mainly get the impression that Lessing was striving to be understood the way she wanted. She was establishing her own legend to control the other legends, and to stop certain kinds of enquiries being pursued, as when Catherine Rihoit put some perceptive questions to her about the relation to the mother and to childhood in both *The Four-Gated City* and *Memoirs of a Survivor*.

When I say, 'she was striving to be understood', what do I mean? To have her books read as she meant them when she wrote them? To have her books understood as she now felt about them? The evolution of her total work understood? To have herself as an 'autobiographical' writer understood? Or to be herself, Doris, understood? As the daughter of a father who has said to me all his life, 'Comprends-moi bien', 'Please understand me', by which he means, 'Agree with me, and if you cannot, then approve of me, and if you cannot, then let me know that you love me', which comes across as a strange mixture of pathos and bullying, I am well aware of the complexities that are at work in anybody, and especially a writer, wanting to be understood. This gets to being machiavellian when reviews and interviews are at stake. For there is a narcissistic dimension to being reviewed. The author keeps hoping for that ideal, loving image of himself/herself, him or herself as projected into the alter ego of the book and reflected back. And is endlessly disappointed.

Are interviews less disappointing, and did Lessing find them so? In a sense, interviews are a peculiar sort of delusion. For the sake of good copy, and of being seen as the gold-digger who did find some ore, the interviewer produces all that love. He or she becomes, for the duration of the interview, the mirror, mirror on the wall that is going to tell the writer he or she is the most beautiful of them all. Nine times out of ten this is killing the hen that lays the golden eggs. Is the Doris Lessing French interviewers met, who they thought looked like a Dutch lady or like Miss Marple, whose Hampstead house could be identified by its marauding cats, the Doris Lessing that wrote *Shikasta*? Proust would have answered no, emphatically. But being interviewed, and very much in control of the situation, Lessing could also ensure she would be quoted, and use the opportunity to put forward her own version of her childhood or her present thoughts about women and feminism.[2] She could smudge the media photokits.

For perhaps she suffered from the way she was manufactured

and sold in France. She was presented from the first as gold bullion, 'Nobélisable', and that knowledge all French reviewers brought to their reading of the, as it turned out, aptly named, *Carnet d'or*. She was hailed as 'the greatest woman writer since Virginia Woolf', 'the greatest living English writer'. It was seeing how she had been sold as a (golden) personality in France that made real to me her complaints about the book industry and what had led her to devise the Jane Somers hoax. In one of her French interviews she quotes an American publisher who said he could not take *Jane Somers* because 'there was nothing to sell'. Meaning, no marketable image behind the book. Being the kind of writer that she is, with her preoccupation with the transpersonal, Lessing must have had problems with that burdensome media double, Doris Lessing. She must also have wanted to know afresh what it was like to have her text received as a text instead of the projection of a name. So, she acted out the role that the critics had mapped out for her, projecting both authorship and autobiography on to a fictitious author, Jane Somers. She turned the mirrors on the critics, giving them a fictitious diarist and a fictitious autobiography they would perceive as genuine because it would be *sold* as the genuine article. Disguising and distancing her real authorship, maybe she was retrieving her soul, her double? Not so in France of course, where *Les Carnets de Jane Somers* was published under Lessing's name. It gave her, however, a full airing for her views. The hoax was much appreciated, being compared to that of Romain Gary who won the Goncourt prize twice, once under his own name and the second time under the pseudonym Emile Ajar.[3]

In Woolf's *Between the Acts*, the poet, Miss La Trobe, at the end of her pageant about the history of England, has the actors turn mirrors on to the audience to represent the present: much to the displeasure of the audience. I think this is what Lessing was doing with *Jane Somers*, and it is the appropriate thing to do with the critical reception of her work in France. It tells as much about French history 1976–86 as about Lessing herself. Through the reviews you can follow the debates, the climaxing and decline of the women's movement. You can watch how the French construct an 'Anglo-Saxon' writer, good at the detail of human relationships and at the minute observation of objects and landscapes. You can feel the growing conservatism of the eighties, in which Lessing gets praised for being such a finely detailed psychological writer, as in *The Summer Before the Dark* or *A Man and Two Women*, whilst *Shikasta* is portrayed as 'indigestible', 'dense and a tiny bit pontificating', a 'homily', the work of a typically 'Anglo-Saxon' 'proselytising' 'popess'.[4] Psychology rocks no boats . . . Lessing's relation to the present, however, also bothers some reviewers in more interesting ways. Some wonder whether the form of *GN* is sufficiently 'shattered' for it to be a contemporary text, whether the voices of author, narrator and protagonist do not uncomfortably blend at times. The question of Lessing's modernity is posed most searchingly by Alain Bousquet. He says that *GN* and the first four volumes of the *Children of Violence* had made him conceive of Lessing as 'a quiet little lady in the anglo-saxon tradition' who used 'neo-Victorian psychology', but that *La Cité promise* was more startling and allowed other things to happen. It also finally revealed to him, he says, the fundamental flaw in Lessing's work, which is to be *aesthetically* one century behind. The character of Mark Coldridge emblematises this. If he had been a post-Joycean writer he would have wondered *how* to write, instead of why write. The social and political preoccupations in the novel are contemporary with the forties and fifties but the questions are irrelevant, old-fashioned, and there is something gratuitous, a lack of necessity, in Martha's breakdown: it is supposed to be an interiorisation of the atomic age, but the atomic age so far has been less apocalyptic than the novelist says (Bousquet, p. 111).

Alain Bosquet's criticism seems to me to go to the heart of the matter. Lessing needs an apocalypse, personal and/or political, to go through the looking-glass, through the wall, into the blue. The personal apocalypse may be death, madness, the loss of a loved one: its strength and significance, we are always given to understand, are that it is political, corresponds to the nuclear holocaust, signifies the end of a species, of a mode of life, a planet. Its relevance will ultimately depend upon its being true to time – historically true – upon the novels holding up a mirror, concave or otherwise, to the actual world. This is perhaps where my metaphor crashes, but I have to ask: can you do that unless the language in which you write is attuned to the ripples that are actually travelling through the air? Or do we live in an age, and does Lessing feel we live in an age in which, language as communication having truly broken down, approximations will do, silver or copper if not gold, anything that will make do as a coating to turn the pane of glass into a mirror? It is towards those questions that a searching reviewer is moving:

You cannot *not* be moved by Lessing, she induces in us too many identifications, too much sympathy. But you cannot either give yourself wholly to her: there is something lacking there, too many problems are false or posed in the wrong way, her world is too readily without issue, without alternative . . . the writing remains conventional. Reading her, you are both sated and starved, saturated and frustrated.   (Biegelmann, p. 29)

Is the 'starvation', the 'frustration' that the more perceptive French reviewers feel, the mark of an unsolved aesthetic problem – or something chosen, imposed by the writer, a post-modernist device meant to engineer a looking-glass and, because you remain 'frustrated', force you *through* the looking-glass?

Notes

1. See Catherine Rihoit, who also says that Lessing is 'the heir of Joseph Conrad and Graham Greene' (p. 41).
2. Lessing modified her position in after years, becoming more sympathetic in her pronouncements on women: 'I am a feminist and I have always been one, but what I am interested in are the labour conditions, the wages', etc., she explained at some length to Geille (p. 157). She praises the women's presses, and Virago in particular, for the way they have brought to light good fiction written by women.
3. Ivan Nabokov, Lessing's French publisher at Albin Michel's, apparently asked whether Lessing had advised Jane Somers when *The Diary of a Good Neighbour* was sent to him. He was rewarded by being let into the secret. The debate was full, sympathy going to Lessing rather than to her embittered Cape publisher. Famous French pseudonyms were evoked, e.g. Stendhal, alias Henri Beyle, and Caton, alias André Bercoff. Romain Gary won the Goncourt prize with *Les Racines du ciel* in 1956, and again as Emile Ajar for *La Vie devant soi* in 1975. See article by television interviewer Jérôme Garcin.
4. There were particularly hostile reviews of *Shikasta*, but also of *Marriages*. See Gehler (1982, 1983) and Queffélec (1981a, b).

Works Cited

The following articles or interviews, from which quotations are taken, represent only a fraction of Lessing's huge French 'Dossier de presse'. On *The Golden Notebook* alone I have copies of twenty-six articles. Altogether there must be in the region of two hundred entries. All translations are mine.

Bernheim, Cathy. 'La planète de Lessing'. *Arts* 11 December 1981.

Biegelmann, Laurence. 'Nourrir le monde'. *Des Femmes en mouvement hebdo* 20 November 1981: 29.

Bosquet, Alain. 'Doris Lessing et l'Apocalypse'. *Magazine Littéraire* May 1981: 111.

Clédat, Françoise T. In *Sorcières* 7 (1976): 56–7.

Fogel, J. P. 'C'est Lessing qu'on assassine'. *Le Point* 19 October 1981: 35.

Gardin, Jerôme. 'Le Jeu du pseudo'. *L'Evénement du Jeudi* 17–23 January 1985: 84–5.

Gehler, Monique. 'Doris Lessing auteur de SF: Faux mouvement'. *Nouvelles littéraires* 11–17 February 1982: 43.

——. 'Ah que c'est long Lessing'. *Nouvelles littéraires* 19–25 May 1983: 42.

Geille, Annick. 'Doris Lessing: "Mais bien sûr, nous sommes les plus fortes!"'. *Femme* March 1985: 77, 157–8.

Queffélec, Yann. 'Doris Lessing'. *Révolution* 30 October 1981.

——. 'Les Illusions de Doris Lessing'. *Le Nouvel Observateur* 28 December 1981: 65.

Rihoit, Catherine. 'Doris Lessing: à livres ouverts'. *F Magazine* June 1981: 41.

Rocher. 'Pitié pour Lessing'. *Livres de France* December 1981.

Wagener, Françoise. 'Doris Lessing à Paris: "No personal questions"'. *Le Monde* 26 November 1976.

Xénakis, Françoise. 'Le Brouillon du *Carnet d'or*'. *Le Matin* 5 April 1978.

Appendix

INTERVIEWS GIVEN BY LESSING IN FRANCE

The reviews of Lessing's many works that have been translated into French are too numerous for it to be possible to list them in an article this size. However, I include a list of interviews given by Lessing over the period 1976–85 because they give an idea of the frequency of Lessing's interventions on the French scene, her willingness to speak to journalists or be quoted there. The list is in chronological order, which best expresses the concentrated attention paid to Lessing over three periods: 1976, when *The Golden Notebook* first appeared; 1981, which saw the publication of a series of disparate novels (*Shikasta*, *The Summer before the Dark*, etc.); and 1984–5, when the two Jane Somers translations brought the 'jeu du pseudo' into focus.

Wagener, Françoise. 'Doris Lessing à Paris: "No personal questions"'. *Le Monde* 26 November 1976.

Ducout, Françoise. 'Les Secrets de Doris Lessing'. *Elle* 17 January 1977: 15.

——. Françoise. 'Doris Lessing: notre anglaise préférée'. *Elle* 20 February 1978.

Rihout, Catherine. 'Doris Lessing: à livres ouverts'. *F Magazine* June 1981: 41.

Thorpe, Michael. 'Une femme de notre temps: entretien avec Doris Lessing'. tr Christine Jordis. *Le Magazine littéraire* October 1981: 25–8.

Braudeau, Michel. 'Doris Lessing: du marxisme au soufisme'. *L'Express* 25 April–4 May 1981: 178–94 (long and interesting).

Zand, Nicole. 'Un parcours étonnant'. *Le Monde* 18 December 1981: 20–1.

Lévy-Willard, Annette. 'Rencontre avec Doris Lessing'. *Liberation* 24–5 December 1981: 27.

Weyergans, François. 'Rendez-vous avec Doris Lessing'. *Le Matin* 25 December 1981: 18.

Pivot, Bernard. 'Apostrophes': the best-known French literary television show; Lessing was done the honour of being invited singly (there are normally four or five guests) and on Christmas Day. She said several anti-Christmas things. 25 December 1981.

Rosset, Pierrette and Ducout, Françoise. 'Une autre guerre des étoiles'. *Elle* 1 February 1982: 30–1.

Bizot, Elizabeth D. and J. F. 'Comment Doris Lessing a réussi à piéger tous les éditeurs'. *Actuel* December 1984: 138–9.

Lessing, Doris, copyright. 'Doris Lessing: pourquoi j'ai changé de nom'. tr. Marianne Fabvre. *L'Express* 11–17 January 1985: 81–3.

Rousseau, François-Olivier. 'Entretien'. *Le Magazine littéraire* February 1985: 85–9 (long and informative).

Alphant, Marianne. 'Doris Lessing et sa voisine Jane Somers'. *Libération* 28 January 1985: 38.

Geille, Annick. 'Doris Lessing: "Mais bien sûr, nous sommes les plus fortes!"'. *Femme* March 1985: 77, 157–8.

7

The German Doris Lessing: A Mixed [B]Lessing*

MONA KNAPP

Not one, but two Doris Lessings are alive and well in the German language. Political distinctions have determined the constitutions and development of an East and a West Germany since 1949, shortly before Lessing began publishing. Accordingly, teutonic discovery of her works was to take place in one language, but on two sides of the century's largest political barrier. Readers in both the Federal Republic of Germany – the economic and strategic pride of NATO – and in the German Democratic Republic, the pillar of the Warsaw Pact, have a specific, if not entirely accurate, picture of Doris Lessing. These two pictures contradict each other as clearly as do East and West. And where Lessing's publishing history in West Germany has been a long-fused time bomb that turned into one of the most unusual chapters in that country's entire postwar literary history, her works in the East display instead a typical conformity to the GDR's literary–political structure and speak almost paradigmatically for its evolution.

Lessing's impact on West Germany began in earnest only in the mid-1970s and is characterised by three major phases to date: virtual obscurity (but for a small circle of admirers who could read the original texts) until 1978; a frantic flurry of interest and acclaim from 1978 until approximately 1984; a third, more objective, evaluation ushered in by *Canopus* and intensified during critics' and readers' evaluations of 'Jane Somers', *The Good Terrorist* and *The Fifth Child*. This three-step development is paralleled elsewhere in Western Europe, especially in France. A further general characteristic linking Germany to its neighbours is the fact that the

---

* This essay is a revised, updated and enlarged version of 'Lessing on the Continent: How Germany Finally Lost Its Heart'. *The Doris Lessing Newsletter* 10:1 (Spring 1986): 8–9, 13.

113

influence of the international feminist movement and (whether Lessing likes it or not) its beloved classic, *The Golden Notebook*, undeniably initiated her breakthrough there. Feminism, literature and Lessing's name will be forever linked in West Germany, as elsewhere in the West.

Not so in the East. The German Democratic Republic's constitution guarantees women equal rights and precludes, at least officially, the importance of feminism or other minor 'isms' subordinate to the overriding goal of socialism. East German feminism does, of course, exist, constitutional equality notwithstanding. To explore it, however, would more than exceed the bounds of this chapter. In any case, it has had no official impact on Lessing reception, and East German feminist thinkers such as Christa Wolf have, to my knowledge, made no special mention of Lessing or her works.

But before looking at the somewhat stunted West German feminist movement that pulled Lessing to the forefront there during the seventies, let me summarise the conditions of the two German publishing marketplaces. West Germany's literary scene is among the most lively in the world. With over fifty thousand new titles published yearly, the Federal Republic of Germany can boast – despite a relatively small population of some sixty million – the world's third largest publishing industry, following only the USA and the Soviet Union. The country's citizens are among the Western world's most literate and literature-conscious. In keeping with a centuries-long tradition of inferiority complexes regarding their own language and concurrent admiration of French and British culture, German readers are generally well informed about literary developments in other countries. Since the 1950s, it has been a matter of course for successful Anglo-Saxon and other European books to be translated and launched on the West German market. West Germany's reading appetite is so voracious that even the most mediocre books offered by American presses are often lavishly published and generously reviewed there, and it seldom takes longer than one or two years for any moderately successful English-language author to appear on the West German scene. Competition is intense. The supply of literature in translation on this lively free market displays a refreshing (if sometimes overwhelming) heterogeneity, offering everything from Charlotte Brontë to Georgette Heyer.

The East German forum, on the other hand, though now more

liberal than it was twenty years ago, is still a model of state control and ideological filtering. The conditions of literary production there are drastically different from those in the West. Literature in its official form is state-sanctioned and accordingly predictable. In a word, literature affirming the goals of the modern socialist state is propagated, literature that criticises it is suppressed. The Eastern market therefore lacks the plurality, the quirks and surprises characteristic of its Western neighbour. Accordingly, East Germany's picture of Doris Lessing is probably one of the world's most streamlined and unambiguous perceptions of this author.

Her marriage to Gottfried Anton Lessing in 1945 made Doris Lessing, if only briefly, a potential German citizen. She could theoretically have accompanied him home from Africa after the war to take up German citizenship under the ideological system she had, in her Rhodesian political work, espoused. Had Lessing held true to the position stated so eloquently in her essay 'The Small Personal Voice' that socialist commitment is the most ethical source of great literature, she might be a heroine in the East today, despite her scepticism regarding the 'little tracts about progress, the false optimism, the dreadful lifeless products of socialist realism' (*SPV*, p. 13). But Doris Lessing separated from her husband, an outward separation connected no doubt to her gradual inner distantiation from the communist cause: her goal was England, not occupied Germany. In 1949 Gottfried Lessing returned to the freshly founded German Democratic Republic to become a successful state official (he was killed in 1979 by troops of Idi Amin while serving as a GDR ambassador to Uganda). Lessing, in the meantime, made a home in bourgeois England after her divorce and was to join and leave the Communist Party within seven years of her arrival there. During the early years of her career, she was still politically acceptable to the communist government of East Germany. But at that time she was merely an unknown author and minor journalist, not noteworthy enough to play any major role in the artificial construction of politically 'correct' literature and socialist realism, despite her participation in the Writers' Delegation to Moscow in 1952. A volume of her short stories was translated and published by the East German publisher Die Tribüne in 1956 (*Der Zauber ist nicht verkäuflich*: two short stories and three of *Five*'s novellas), but this was to remain Lessing's solitary appearance in East Germany for some time.[1] Lessing's 'desertion' of the Communist Party by 1960 apparently sufficed to make her works unwelcome there for the next twenty years. Even though the first doctoral dissertations ever written on Lessing came out of East Germany (two were completed in Leipzig in 1963), neither her works nor secondary studies on them were readily available there until the mid-1980s. It is amusing, and typical of the rebellious and capricious young Lessing, that she managed to become *persona non grata* almost simultaneously in arch-rightist South Africa (where she was 'prohibited' in the early 1950s) and in the diametrically opposed political climate of socialist East Germany.

Nor did the 1950s and 1960s bring Lessing the recognition in West Germany that one could, according to the given translation and publishing market, have expected. *The Grass Is Singing*, published by Bertelsmann in 1953, only three years after its appearance in England, received a few lukewarm reviews and was subsequently forgotten. It was not until 1980 that it made a comeback, enthusiastically received by readers who were often unaware that it was Lessing's oldest rather than her newest novel. (Indeed, several of its reviewers in 1980 did not even realise that it had been printed previously, and erroneously noted its 'belated' arrival on the scene.) Thus, a subtotal of Lessing's visibility in both Germanies during the first twenty-five years of her career produces (comparable in this respect to Spain) a balance of plus or minus zero.

The political reasons for Lessing's delayed arrival in the East, as noted above, are transparent enough. Less transparent are the reasons for West Germany's long hesitation. Coincidence, of course, may have played a role: some authors catch on, others don't until the time is ripe. Almost certainly, however, the decisions made by publishers and readers of Lessing's texts during the 1950s were also influenced by political conditions. In 1953, when *The Grass Is Singing* would have paved the way to Lessing's success in West Germany, readers there were still very busy with established authors they had missed between 1933 and 1945. A short eight years had passed since they had regained access to world literature, and they concentrated not only on the works of their own exiles, such as Thomas Mann, Berthold Brecht and Carl Zuckmayer, but also on foreign writers banned by the Nazi regime, notably Faulkner and Hemingway, as well as Camus and the French surrealists and existentialists. The political situation had barely stabilised, with the Federal Republic founded in 1949 and Konrad Adenauer's Christian Democratic government just gaining ground. The problems of colonialism in Africa were a long way off. As for racism, the Germans hardly had to look to the British colonies for material. Their own efforts to come to terms with National Socialist atrocities were to extend well into the coming decades.

At the same time, the Cold War was on. West Germany, anxious to strengthen its Western alliance, was almost as paranoid as the United States regarding the 'Soviet threat'. Doris Lessing was a Communist in 1953, and the translation of her first novel appeared at a time when any kind of socialism was often simplistically 'equated with Stalinism and therefore appeared intolerable' (Drewitz).[2] None the less, West German publishers did not give up on Lessing totally after *The Grass Is Singing*. Bertelsmann produced a volume of short stories (*Die andere Frau; The Other Woman*) in 1954. But the pro-communist tendency of *Retreat to Innocence*, printed in England in 1956, was probably the factor that put Lessing on ice in Cold War West Germany. Only a few years later, during the 1960s, the country was to develop a dynamic literary–political pluralism that would easily have absorbed what Lessing was producing, but by that time the boat had apparently been missed: with the single exception of *Play With a Tiger's* moderately successful run in Dortmund in 1964, Lessing's name remained virtually unknown in West Germany until the late 1970s.

Early in 1975, the *Frankfurter Allgemeine Zeitung*, a major newspaper, featured *The Summer Before the Dark* in sequels. This novel then appeared in book form published by Rowohlt as part of their large-scale effort to establish contemporary female authors in affordable German translations. Despite the professed feminist intentions, however, Rowohlt's *neue frau* series has been criticised repeatedly for trivialising women's literature, and *Summer* did not help its (or Lessing's) image. *Summer* received either a polite nod or, in places, a good scolding for its naive depiction of women in the workforce (Kurz and Schuh). Since it fails to expose, in fact deliberately glosses over, the conditions encountered by most employed women, especially middle-aged, untrained ones like Kate Brown, it could hardly appeal to feminist activists, and it was not well-enough received to give Lessing's name anything but marginal visibility.

In 1978, however, *The Golden Notebook* followed, and Lessing became a celebrity almost overnight. Like American readers fourteen years earlier, German readers perceived *The Golden Notebook* as a guiding manual and source of moral support for a budding social movement. In the late 1970s, West Germany's female and feminist readers were still largely in the process of consciousness-raising. The history of feminism on German ground is long and complicated (see Schenk; Weigel). German feminism suffered a unique and devastating setback during the National Socialist regime (see Millett, pp. 217–29), from which it was slow to recover: indeed, today West Germany is still a patriarchal stronghold. The entire public school system, for example, presupposes a non-career mother who is available at home constantly: children are released regularly around noon (and quite often without notice at mid-morning), and a parent, usually the mother, is responsible for monitoring *over 50 per cent* of the total school work at home during the afternoon.[3] While German feminist groups did begin to organise – inspired by examples from the Unites States – in the 1970s, they met with strong opposition in a society structured so tightly around patriarchal principles, hierarchy and conformity. As far as literature is concerned, the first book to reach and mobilise women readers in appreciable numbers was Verena Stefan's *Häutungen* in 1975 ('Shedding Skins'). This is an autobiographical account of dubious literary merit describing one woman's decision to live without men, whom she equates with sexist degradation in general. The mid-seventies saw the founding of feminist journals (*Frauen und Film* in 1974, *Frauenoffensive* journal and publishing house in 1975, *Emma* in 1977) and remedial reading of foreign authors such as Kate Millett, Germaine Greer and Simone de Beauvoir. German feminists such as Alice Schwarzer began to emerge into the public eye (Schwarzer is still today the major spokeswoman for feminism, even though she committed the traitorous act of getting married in 1988). Women began to see themselves as a collective force and their literature as a consciousness-raising tool. In short, by the late 1970s, West German feminists had reached a point in theory and organisation that had been attained approximately ten years earlier by their American counterparts across the Atlantic (where, incidentally, the militant fervour had long subsided and the post-feminist yuppy generation was already being raised). German feminists at this point very much needed identifiable role models and writers with strong voices: into this climate Lessing's *Golden Notebook* was launched. It was the right book at the right time, and although it did not achieve singular cult-status as *the* feminist book (an honour permanently claimed, it seems, by Verena Stefan's *Häutungen*), it did attract readers in great numbers and associated the power of Lessing's social visions with the feminist movement. (This despite the fact that Lessing's prose does not translate well into German: the final product is often wooden and lacking the inimitable subtlety of the original.) The criticisms that could have been levelled at it from a mature feminist point of view – and have indeed been voiced in the meantime by British and American scholars – did not arise in West Germany. Instead, the women's movement saw the *Golden Notebook's* author as a woman who dared to cross the borders of purely female experience and 'let women become human beings', as stated by the reviewer in *Emma* (Lander, p. 53). This journal (a somewhat more radical equivalent to *Ms.* in that it makes the feminist movement accessible to the average newsstand-peruser) has regularly reviewed every Lessing release and made Lessing's name part of the reading canon for West German readers interested in the women's movement.

Emma makes clear from the outset that it would be too simplistic to label Lessing *a* feminist author. German feminists took very seriously Lessing's own disclaimer of feminist intention in her 1972 foreword – and perhaps it was this very ambiguity that made the book appealing to so many. Every reader can somehow find her own problems reflected here: 'For me, the book is mainly about the difficulties of being a woman writer' (Lander, p. 53). At a time when women writers in contemporary West German fiction were just beginning to see themselves as something more than isolated deviants, Anna Wulf was a model. In addition, the feminist literary forum in Germany in 1978 was new, heterogeneous, experimental and at times amateurish. It had made many readers hungry for works with the polish of world-class literature:

> At present – the late 1970s – *The Golden Notebook* is more interesting and more relevant than most of the other texts on the market written about women by women. Lessing's Anna is smarter and more experienced, or at least more open to experience than most other contemporary female protagonists. (Barnouw, p. 601; my translation)

The international women's movement, then, conditioned the success of *The Golden Notebook* and brought Lessing to Germany: phase two had begun. As was to be expected, admirers of *The Golden Notebook* immediately demanded more translations. Through the efforts of eleven translators to date, they began to appear rapidly, though not always in logical order. Several publishing houses have become involved: one book each is featured by Rowohlt, Reclam, Diogenes (Switzerland) and Wagenbach, and the Deutscher Tasch-enbuch Verlag began publishing authorised paperback editions of *Children of Violence* in 1987. But basically Lessing is 'shared' by Klett-Cotta and Fischer-Goverts, two huge publishing concerns. They produce, in fact, some rather droll competition between themselves, such as the simultaneous publication in autumn 1986 of two works originally published twenty-five years apart: Fischer's *The Terrorist* (1985) and Klett-Cotta's *In Pursuit of the English* (1960). Well at least, one reviewer consoled his reader, they are both about a commune(!).

By 1978 Lessing's works were, of course, so voluminous that there was some doubt where to begin. Klett-Cotta, in fact, had owned the rights to *The Golden Notebook* since 1976, but had actually delayed its publication while putting together the first volume of Lessing's short stories. One very shrewd decision was the publication of *Martha Quest* in 1981. This readable traditional novel is appetising fare for a wide readership, but also appealing to feminists, who received it warmly. And since nothing goes against the German grain more than getting just one part of a pentalogy when everyone else has all five parts, readers demanded the rest of *Children of Violence*: 'Now that we've finally gained access to Lessing's works, we just can't get enough' (van Winsen; my translation). The plea for sequels persisted until *The Four-Gated City*, published in 1984, fifteen years after its British debut, was finally greeted with a satisfied sigh.[4]

With similar possessiveness, West German journalists often subtly 'lay claim' to Lessing: it is almost standard procedure to emphasise that she shares the last name of one of the great classical writers, Gotthold Ephraim Lessing. One critic even ventured the assertion that she chose this name by design, as a literary status symbol. Not infrequently, bibliographical references to her works and those of G. E. Lessing are mixed or confused. In fairness, though, even if Martha *Hesse's* last name is a clear allusion to this 'name problem', it is doubtful that Lessing has any particular relationship to Germany. Her ambivalence toward postwar Ger-many is wonderfully captured in 'The Eye of God in Paradise', but otherwise the country plays no significant role in her works. She does not, she says, read contemporary German writers. They do read her, though: she is named by authors such as Ingeborg Drewitz, Angelika Mechtel, Gabriele Wohmann and others as a colleague to read and learn from.

Lessing's growing popularity was additionally boosted by her tour in 1981 ('A triumphal procession through our country' – Schostack), during which she held question-and-answer sessions in Stuttgart, Frankfurt, Hamburg, Berlin and other cities. German readers felt 'understood' by Lessing and found their problems reflected intelligently and sympathetically by her books. Numerous interviewers stressed her motherliness and wisdom, as well as her ladylike British manners:

> There she sat in an armchair like Rumpelstiltskin, a small, firm person, her grey, centreparted hair pulled tightly into a bun, beaming beneficence like a fairy godmother . . . one could almost take her for a Swabian parson's wife. (Schostack; my translation)

In this hectic second phase of Lessing's reception, readers discovered everything from *Particularly Cats* to *Shikasta*, often in a motley concoction. It is interesting that the *Katzenbuch* (*Particularly Cats*), published in 1981 and now in its fourth printing, was received with more warmhearted enthusiasm than any other volume. It is cited repeatedly as Lessing's most delightful, most personal, most poetic and endearing text, the 'best introduction to her work' (Arbogast). Not the first time, one might add, that the German mentality has been observed to harbour more sympathy for the plight of animals than for that of human beings.

German sympathy for our author, in any event, was made official when Lessing received the Shakespeare prize of the Hamburger Stiftung in 1982, a high distinction accompanied by considerable publicity. Publishers now were busy filling in the older works and keeping up with Lessing's unexpectedly prolific production of the *Canopus* novels. Since the German publication of *Children of Violence* (1981–4) overlapped partially with that of *Canopus* (1983–5), the unsuspecting reader endeavouring to discover one author must surely at times have felt she was discovering two. And not always to her pleasure. Readers 'primed' for more Lessing by novels such as *A Proper Marriage* (1982) were less than thrilled by *Shikasta* the following year.

The *Canopus* series, indeed, fundamentally changed Lessing's standing with the press. Most reviewers granted her good intentions but poor results in using science fiction techniques. Reviews were increasingly sceptical, though they applauded enthusiastically the thematic focus on Good and Evil and Lessing's optimistic declaration that evil *can* be conquered. *Shikasta's* critique of modern civilisation was treated with due respect, as were certain aspects of *Marriages*. The *Sirian Experiments*, however, could hardly keep reviewers awake, and neither *Planet 8* nor the *Sentimental Agents* could improve matters. The press, having impatiently demanded more Lessing only a few years before, now began to groan under the weight of her verbose style. One writer finally ventured to suggest that instead of reading *Canopus*, we should all consider making a visit to the local planetarium. The effect would be approximately the same, and we would be left with hours of free time to read books with 'more concentrated and painstaking style, and less affectation' (Mayer).

By the mid-eighties, when the *Canopus*-Lessing had come out of the closet of realism, many readers decided they'd had enough. Phase three began as even booksellers found her books resting a bit heavily on the shelves, 'thick and fat, as if immovable . . . no one buys them anymore' (Widmann). Clearly, the time was ripe for a new new Lessing. Having been both an unknown and a fad, she thus graduated to the solid ranks of established living authors who thrive on despite their good and their bad reviews, their circles of fans and mudslingers. The Jane Somers ruse was performed simultaneously in German translation and aroused, predictably, the scorn of journalists, who found it devious and manipulative. Some consequently rejected the books as artificial social commentary, and unappetising to read besides. Others, reflecting the positive reaction of Germany's large contingency of older readers, applauded and suggested that *The Good Neighbour* was one of Lessing's very finest books.

Events of the most recent years have been viewed by Lessing's public with a new subjectivity, not to say coolness. Lessing was invited to speak in June 1986, at the prestigious Akademie der Künste in Berlin, hosted by the well-known Germanist and publicist Walter Höllerer. She collided so hopelessly with her host – she was described in *Der Tagesspiegel*, one of Berlin's major newspapers, as irritating him with 'blah-blah' – that he broke off the interview and left further questioning to the audience. A Berlin production of *Each His Own Wilderness* in autumn 1987 received unusually heterogeneous reviews, which variously hailed its timelessness and booked it as a big disappointment.

Germany's mixed feelings in assessing Lessing are further demonstrated by the reception of *The Good Terrorist*, published a year after the English original with the word 'good' conspicuously missing from the title *Die Terroristin*. The reaction from the feminist left was devastating. *Emma* left behind its tradition of benevolent praise through which *The Golden Notebook* and *Children of Violence* had been recommended to so many readers. Its review of *The Terrorist* was harsh and scornful:

> The publisher tells us that in *The Terrorist* Lessing has returned to earth. She must have had a hard fall. And received a bad blow on the head besides. If only she had stayed behind the walls, in her other realms! . . . This novel is probably the worst book to be written by any professional author in recent years.   (Strobl; my translation)

Alice's feminine habit of bursting into tears at every turn, like her general devotion to housework and cooking, gave West German feminists occasion to finally strip the kid gloves they had used for Lessing's previous publications. No longer is she admired as a source of advice for novice feminists, rather she is scoffed at for having nothing better to say in 'Auntie Doris's Advice Column' than that radical change in the world is primarily a prank for spoiled middle-class children. She gives the truly exploited members of society 'the choice between flipping out and dying' (Strobl) – but denies them any hope of actual social change. Lessing was also criticised by numerous reviewers for her mushy approach to politics as a hodge-podge of health-food nuts and urban guerrillas. One reviewer found the book 'offensive in its nearly criminal neglect of the programmatical, sociological, psychological and political motivations of the "New Left"' (Wackwitz; my translation). Others, however, found it 'cleanly researched' and highly competent (Stromberg).

Initial reactions to *The Fifth Child*, which appeared first in newspaper sequels during summer 1988, in the *Frankfurter Allgemeine Zeitung* and in book form the following autumn, are ambivalent. *The Fifth Child*'s author is recognised for the perfection of narrative technique that 'drives the reader forward, disbelieving and shocked, from one page to the next' (Deutsche Presse Agentur).

But she is also criticised for her lack of compassion and for an auctorial viewpoint that could, the same journalist theorises, too easily metamorphose into an espousal of concentration camps and euthanasia for misfits such as Ben Lovatt. Diversity has also been the watchword of the German scholarly community, which has approached Lessing from a large variety of ideological/method-ological directions.[5] None of these has been dominant. Deconstruction has had little influence, and even feminism has remained largely restricted to popular journals and newspapers, rather than influencing scholarship. It is fair to say that both scholars and general readers in West Germany in the mid-1980s are trying to comprehend Lessing's multifaceted thematic and ideological development without pinning her down to any single dimension.

In contrast, East Germany has managed, in the course of the 1980s, to 'reconstruct' an image of Doris Lessing that can be officially condoned. Gradual loosening of restrictions during the 1970s, in conjunction with increasing recognition of Lessing's early anti-bourgeois works, made her 'revival' possible, within limits. In 1987, I found three Lessing volumes available to interested East German readers: *Hunger* (*Hunger*; Leipzig, 1984), *Winter in July* (*Winter im Juli*; Berlin, 1984) and *The Grass Is Singing* (*Afrikanische Tragödie*; Berlin, second edition, 1987). Scholarly contributions in established journals (Wienhold; Sander) gave an official placet to the Eastern picture of Lessing, based cautiously on the anti-bourgeois segment of her youth. It looks something like this: Doris Lessing had the intelligence to become a communist at a young age, the good sense to marry a German communist, and the courage to speak out against the capitalist regime in South Africa. Unfortunately, anti-communist propaganda and repressive measures by the government forced her political group to disband. She nevertheless remained progressive and continued to attack colonialist capitalism for some years. Her influential exposé of racism and corruption in South Africa is her greatest achievement: works such as *Hunger* depict the hunger of all humanity for economic justice. Her African stories show how the historical/material conditions of colonialism destroy the moral centre of society. The young Lessing, opponent of apartheid, can be fully embraced as an example of moral/intellectual righteousness.

Interestingly enough, Lessing's later works are integrated into this picture with the argument that they continue to demonstrate the ruinous effects of bourgeois existence, whether intentionally or not. The *Golden Notebook*, which has been the object of Marxist criticism in the East (Vassilieva), is seen as a self-torturing attempt to solve the ideological conflict between communist commitment and bourgeois existence with a third, highly privatised, of course untenable alternative. No wonder, the Eastern sources imply, she is mad. No wonder the bourgeois reader loves this book more than any other. Novels such as *Briefing* and *Summer* prove even more clearly that decent human personalities cannot possibly remain intact under the degenerative influence of capitalist society. The 'proof' is not clear enough, however, to justify making these novels available to readers in the East. Therefore Lessing's early works will probably, at least for the foreseeable future, be the only ones officially condoned there.

Many Western readers will probably agree that, if a reader is to receive only *one* of the many Lessings, this is not the worst possible choice. It is an irony of ideology that the hot-headed young idealist who believed in the moral and emancipatory potential of literature and who plainly hated the capitalist regime is the origin of Lessing's fame *in both East and West*. In the GDR, the 'young Red' Lessing will live on, artificially perpetuated by government guidelines that find her most acceptable that way. In the West, where the majority of her fans and devotees were first captivated by her youthfully outspoken socialism, I suspect that many of them still privately treasure this Lessing most. The mystic, the sci-fi dilettante and Lessing's other protean forms we accept, analyse, interpret. Perhaps, in the end, it is the strident rebel with a social cause whom we really love.

Acknowledgements

For extensive and invaluable help with my research I would like to express grateful appreciation to the newspaper archive collection of the Dortmund City Library (Zeitungsausschnittsammlung der Stadtbücherei Dortmund); equal thanks go to my colleagues Henryk Kellermann, Thomas and Evi Rietzschel, Paul Schlueter, and the archives of *Emma*.

Notes

1. The short story 'The Other Woman' was also anthologised for East German readers in the collection *Prosa und Lyrik der britischen Inseln*.
2. Drewitz, herself a renowned progressive writer who died in 1987, was the only critic I found who made the explicit connection between Lessing's political views and Germany's politics during the Stalin era. All others puzzle on Lessing's obscurity as an unsolved mystery.
3. Though West German women are granted equal rights by law, they are far from having equal representation in government. Were the rate of increase in female representation to continue as in the decade from 1978 to 1988, a recent calculation showed, it would take another 300 years to achieve equality.
4. See Knapp for more details on the German reception of Lessing's individual works.
5. See Dahlhaus Beilner, Kellermann and Spiegel for three products of the lively dissertational and scholarly activity on Lessing. The Spring 1989 issue of the *Doris Lessing Newsletter* was devoted exclusively to the German reception.

Works Cited

Arbogast, Herbert. Review of *Particularly Cats*. *Rheinischer Merkur*, 5 October 1984.

Barnouw, Dagmar. '"People are like other People": Doris Lessing'. *Merkur* (1979): 599–605.

Dahlhaus Beilner, Barbara. *Wahnsinn: Symptom und Befreiung*. Amsterdam: Verlag B. R. Grüner, 1984.

Deutsche Presse-Agentur. '"Das fünfte Kind" wird zum Alptraum für seine Familie'. *Ruhr-Nachrichten* 201 (29 August 1988).

'"Die ächste Eiszeit steht bevor": Die britische Schriftstellerin Doris Lessing sprach in der Akademie der Künste'. *Der Tagenspiel* 12:378 (8 June 1986): 4.

Drewitz, Ingeborg. 'Nachdenken über Doris Lessing'. *Courage* 6 (11 November 1981): 26–8.

Kellermann, Henryk. *Die Weltanschauung im Romanwerk von Doris Lessing*. Frankfurt am Main, Berne and New York: Peter Lang Verlag, 1985.

Knapp, Mona. 'Lessing on the Continent: How Germany Finally Lost its Heart'. *Doris Lessing Newsletter* 10.1 (1986): 8–9, 13.

Kurz, Ingrid and Franz Schu. 'Die Königin der Dolmetscher. Zu Doris Lessings Vorstellung von Arbeitswelt in ihrem Roman "Der Sommer vor der Dunkelheit"'. *Presse* 11078 (16/17 February 1985): 35.

Lander, Jeanette. 'Ihr goldenes Notizbuch'. *Emma* (November 1978): 50–3.

Lessing, Doris. *A Small Personal Voice*. Ed. Paul Schlueter. New York: Vintage, 1975.

Mayer, Susanne. 'Versteinerte Vernunft. Die strapaziöe und voluminöse Lehrdichtung der südafrikanischen Schriftstellerin Doris Lessing'. *Die Zeit* 49 (30 November 1984): 14.

Millett, Kate: *Sexual Politics*. New York: Doubleday, 1970.
Prosa und Lyrik der britischen Inseln. Berlin and Weimar: Aufbau-Verlag, 1968.
Sander, Hans-Jochen. 'Doris Lessing: Winter im Juli'. *Weimarer Beiträge* 32 (1986): 481–91.
Schenk, Herrad: *Die feministische Herausforderung. 150 Jahre Frauenbewegung in Deutschland*. Munich: Beck, 1980.
Schostack, Renate. 'Gegen jede Gehirnwäsche. Ein Gespräch mit der Schriftstellerein Doris Lessing'. *Frankfurter Allgemeine Zeitung* 254 (2 November 1981).
Spiegel, Rotraut. *Doris Lessing: The Problem of Alienation and the Form of the Novel*. Frankfurt am Main and Berne: Peter Lang, 1980.
Stefan, Verena. *Häutungen. Autobiografische Aufzeichnungen, Gedichte, Träume, Analysen*. Munich: Frauenoffensive, 1975.
Strobl, Ingrid. 'Tante Doris' Weisheiten'. *Emma* (November 1986): 36.
Stromberg, Kyra. 'Terrorismus auf englisch'. *Süddeutsche Zeitung* 31 (7/8 February 1987): 4.
Vassilieva, I. 'Liberated Women in Fiction and in Life: Tradition and Reality Today'. *Twentieth Century Literature: A Soviet View*. Moscow: Moscow Publishing House, 1982. 327–9.
Wackwitz, Stephan. 'Eine heilige Johanna der Hinterhöfe'. *Stuttgarter Zeitung* 226 (1 October 1986): 40.
Weigel, Sigrid. *Die Stimme der Medusa. Schreibweisen in der Gegenwartsliteratur von Frauen*. Dülmen-Hiddingsel: tende, 1987.
Widmann, Arno. 'Vom Nachttisch geräumt'. *Die Tageszeitung* 2287 (18 August 1987): 13.
Wienhold, Christa. 'Doris Lessing und Afrika'. *Zeitschrift für Anglistik und Amerikanistik* 32 (1984): 128–39.
van Winsen, Christa. 'Später Ruhm in deutschen Landen. Eine längst fällige Begegnung mit Doris Lessing und ihrem Werk'. *Stuttgarter Zeitung* (24 October 1981): 53.

8

Doris Lessing in the Mi[d]st[s] of Ideology: The Spanish Reading*

FERNANDO GALVÁN REULA

A great deal of the fiction published in Spain each year is a product of translations, and certainly novels in the English language constitute a good percentage of the total. Among twentieth-century British novelists, James Joyce, D. H. Lawrence, Joseph Conrad, Virginia Woolf, George Orwell and Graham Greene are the most popular and best known by the general reading public, followed by more recent authors, such as Lawrence Durrell, William Golding, Anthony Burgess, Iris Murdoch and Doris Lessing. However, the case of Lessing is rather peculiar, because although she achieved some renown in the later seventies with the translations of *The Golden Notebook* and the first volumes of the *Children of Violence* series, her reception before and after that date has been weak. She is not taught at high-school level, and only a few universities include her work in the curriculum (there are as yet no women's studies courses in Spanish universities); this is due perhaps to the fact that she is mainly seen, on the one hand, as an 'old fashioned' by-product of the feminist movement and, on the other, paradoxically, as a superficial, conventional woman writer who has abandoned and betrayed her earlier committed way of writing.

In spite of Lessing's emphatic opposition and multiple statements to the contrary, she seems to have been seen, alas, by most readers (until very recently at least) as the author of a single book (*The Golden Notebook*) or a collection of novels that discuss the role of women in comtemporary society. Her development as a 'sci-fi'

<hr />

* This essay is a revised and enlarged version of 'The Spanish Confusion: the Reception of Doris Lessing in Spain', originally published in the *Doris Lessing Newsletter* 11.1 (Spring 1987): 3–4, 12.

writer and her latest return to a more 'realistic' kind of narrative
are practically unknown to the majority of readers: almost no echo
of the debate on the *Canopus in Argos* series or the Jane Somers
affair has surfaced in the press or reached the general reader
(*Shikasta* was translated in 1986, seven years after its original
publication, and *The Diary of a Good Neighbour* late in 1987, after
the Spanish and Catalan versions of *The Good Terrorist*).

The great discovery of Lessing's fiction in Spain took place about
1978, when *The Golden Notebook* was translated – in the same year
as the German version and just two years after the French
translation, for which Lessing was awarded the Prix Medici (1976).
Other translations had appeared as early as 1965, when Seix Barral
of Barcelona (Lessing's usual publisher in Spain in the sixties and
seventies) had brought out *In Pursuit of the English* and, later, *A
Man and Two Women* (1967), *The Grass Is Singing* (1968), *Martha
Quest* (1973), *Briefing for a Descent into Hell* (1974) and *The Summer
Before the Dark* (1974). Nevertheless, Lessing was virtually unknown
to the common reader. Only after the success of *The Golden Notebook*
in the late seventies did her work begin to be widely discussed in
literary journals and newspapers. Translations suddenly in-
creased,[1] so that the Spanish reader of the eighties can find most
of her novels and short stories in every bookshop. Lessing's trips
to Madrid and Barcelona, in April 1983 and March 1987, enlarged
her reading public and were also a sort of test that measured the
level of knowledge about the novelist in Spain.

The six works translated before *The Golden Notebook* had a cool
reception; few traces of their impact are visible in the great literary
reviews and newspapers. They appeared before 1975, a date that
has become significant in the cultural life of Spain because it marks
more than the death of Franco, the end of dictatorship and the
arrival of democracy; it also marks a change of attitude towards
foreign influences that in the case of Lessing is highly relevant. A
good example of prevailing ignorance about Lessing is shown by
the retranslations of some major works that had been published
before *The Golden Notebook* but which nobody remembered. *The
Grass Is Singing, Briefing for a Descent into Hell* and *The Summer Before
the Dark* were translated again in 1984, 1985 and 1984, respectively;
the other titles (with the exception of *In Pursuit of the English*) were
reissued, although some critics thought that the reissues were new
and fresh translations. What has happened with Lessing's works
is not uncommon, however, since double and triple translations

are not rare in the confusing Spanish book-market.

During her trip to Spain in 1983, Lessing herself must have been amazed by the discovery that some of her best books had not been translated. When she was interviewed by Maruja Torres for the newspaper *El País*, she said that of all her works the ones she preferred were the ones ignored by the Spanish reader (she meant *Briefing for a Descent into Hell* and *The Memoirs of a Survivor*). *Briefing*, however, had been published in Spain in 1974, and *Memoirs*, in 1979, according to the information given by Nissa Torrents in her interview with Lessing in the left-wing weekly *La Calle* (1980).[2] The response from the publishers of *Memoirs* was immediate – about two months after Lessing's visit they issued a pocket edition of the novel. Two years later *Briefing* was again translated. Perhaps these new editions were prompted by Lessing's words, but new translations of other novels were also made. *The Grass Is Singing*, for example, received a second translation, in spite of the outstanding reputation of its first translator in 1968, José María Valverde (the translator of a much-praised version of *Ulysses* and Eliot's poems); and *The Summer Before the Dark*, translated in 1974 by Francesco Parcerisas, was translated again in 1984 by J. Manuel Alvarez Flórez. *Martha Quest* was not retranslated but merely reissued by Argos-Vergara in 1980, following the success of *A Proper Marriage* (1979). Nobody seemed to notice that the 1980 edition was the 'old' version of 1973. On the contrary, reviewers complained about the illogical order of publication: first *A Proper Marriage* (1979), then *Martha Quest* (1980), which was immediately followed by *A Ripple from the Storm* (1980), *Landlocked* (1980) and *The Four-Gated City* (1982).

This confusing panorama shows that Lessing was well known only in very specialised circles – mostly universities and also some serious literary journals – which kept up to date. But in predemocratic Spain, that is, before 1975, the rigours of censorship and the great difficulties involved in translating writers who were presumed to be communists or leftists meant that 'up to date' could very well be a delay of ten years; and hence the confusion in the translations and reception.

Nevertheless, we find in the bibliography of this period a provocative treatment of Lessing's works in Cándido Pérez Gállego's scholarly study of the generation of the 'Angry Young Men': *Literatura y rebeldía en la Inglaterra actual* (1968). Pérez Gállego examines *In Pursuit of the English*, *The Grass Is Singing*, the first three novels of *Children of Violence* and *The Golden Notebook*, as well as the short stories in *Five*, *The Habit of Loving* and *A Man and Two Women*, and the plays. This is the first and only time (as far as I know) that *Mr Dolinger*, *Each His Own Wilderness*, *The Truth About Billy Newton* and *Play With a Tiger* are discussed in Spanish; the emphasis of the analysis and interpretation of Pérez Gállego is sociological, relating these works to Lessing's early political and artistic commitment in *Declaration*. He compares *In Pursuit* with Orwell's *The Road to Wigan Pier* and traces the development of this commitment up to *The Golden Notebook*, whose formal experiments are brilliantly analysed, but whose conclusion may seem peculiar today: 'We find in *The Golden Notebook* one of the summits of the movement of the "Angry Young Men"' (Gállego, p. 112). Although this vision has been openly rejected by Lessing herself, who explains that her inclusion in *Declaration* was a consequence of Murdoch's refusal to contribute to that collective work, Pérez Gállego's reading is generally sound, being based on the original texts (and so avoiding the usual fallacies we encounter in other critics of this time).

An example of contemporary opinions on Lessing in the sixties is offered by the well-known reviewer of foreign novels for the literary monthly *Insula*, Domingo Pérez Minik, who includes Lessing in his book *Introductión a la novela inglesa actual* (1968) under the label of 'Angry Young Men', with comments on *In Pursuit* and 'The Eye of God in Paradise', but no further reference to her later (or previous) career (these were the only titles available in Spanish at the time). For Pérez Minik, then, Lessing was in 1968 still the topical political writer of the fifties. Even in 1973, in another book, *La novela extranjera en España*, in which he collects his contributions to *Insula* and other literary reviews, this critic talks about Lessing as a 'woman novelist' and complains in a typically anti-feminist attitude about the large number of women who 'find entertainment' today in writing. He asserts that her best novels, those in the pentalogy, are not known in Spain, and concludes with a rather dismissive judgement:

> Doris Lessing does not write masterpieces like Jane Austen, Dorothy Richardson, and Virginia Woolf. Nor did she invent a literary style to give her creations an eternal value. Her narrative seems to reach only the category of the realistic testimony of a determinate society.   (Pérez Minik, 1973, p. 183)

The power of this cliché is reflected in the fact that even after the publication of *The Golden Notebook*, Pérez Minik continues with this kind of classification. On the occasion of the edition in 1979 of *A Proper Marriage*, for example, he still places Lessing with provincial English literature of the fifties, in a direct line with the great nineteenth-century masters (Pérez Minik, 1980). He adds that although the novelist has attacked the establishment, she has never abandoned it, since the British establishment has been able to adapt to her critiques(!). The description of the colonial world and the ideological position of this novel leads him to say that 'Doris Lessing repeats herself in her way of writing; she has no other way . . . her literary forms are taken from the Fabian novelists, from John Galsworthy to Arnold Bennett'. These considerations about the form of her novels and the 'old-fashioned' models Lessing follows in her fiction contrast with his judgement of her moral views as very contemporary and advanced. His final indictment is really very hard: 'Our novelist is a plain woman with fixed ideas and the unequivocal attitude of a conventional narrator. And that is no offence in the case of Doris Lessing.' Pérez Minik, ignoring *The Golden Notebook* (translated two years earlier), is obviously contemplating Lessing at the end of the seventies as a member of the 'Angry Young Men' generation who has not changed her style or preoccupations.

Unfortunately, Pérez Minik's vision is not exceptional in this 'first period' of criticism on Lessing in Spain. I have quoted him extensively because – as the president of the jury of professional critics that awards a prestigious prize – he seems to me a good representative of the general opinion about the novelist in this country, at least before her visit in 1983. Journalists were probably shocked, when they interviewed her, to meet a person who did not agree with their preconceptions, those shaped by Pérez Minik. Perhaps as a consequence of that 'shock' when meeting the 'real' Lessing, a new understanding of the complexities of the writer began to emerge.

The translation of *A Proper Marriage* makes an excellent case study of the reception of Lessing in 1979–80, when she was starting to be well known in this country. The novel was a sort of bestseller, in spite of the twenty-five years that had passed since its first edition, and was widely reviewed and discussed in literary journals and major newspapers. Pérez Minik's topical vision was accompanied by other confusing analyses from critics who had suddenly discovered at the end of the seventies a novel and a writer of the early fifties. Antonio Blanch, for example, writing for *Reseña de literatura, arte y espectáculos*,referred to the 'simplistic treatment' of situations and characters as well as to the predominant ideological dimension of the novel that turned it, in his opinion, into a thesis novel. Pedro Fernaud, however, reviewing it for the weekly left-wing *Triunfo*, saw it as 'a detailed description of the values, ways and customs of a society . . . a "novel of manners"', And the famous woman writer, and feminist researcher, Carmen Martín Gaite offered her readers in *Diario 16* an acrid account of the novel under the title 'The Dangers of Dogmatism' (p. 20). She expressed her disagreement with the way (excessively insistent) Lessing tackled so many things 'perfectly known to all of us'. That is probably true when Martín Gaite says it, since she is writing at a moment (1979) when Spain, four years after the end of dictatorship, is already familiar with feminism and political struggles within the left, but she seems totally ignorant about the date of the original book: was it really so twenty-five years earlier, when Lessing wrote the novel?

For Martín Gaite, moreover, Lessing does not possess the virtue of making allusions, of selecting, but is better prepared to preach, to attract 'unconditional support from an audience that is already inclined to think, to condemn, and to judge like her'; this means, for the Spanish novelist, that Lessing is unable to lead her readers towards a fiction that is valid *per se*: 'her characters, both when they talk and when they reflect, are almost always expressing . . . in an excessively obvious manner, the author's ideology' (p. 20). Martín Gaite also mentions *The Golden Notebook* in her review, and although she finds it more suggestive than *A Proper Marriage*, she believes it is as deficient in style and dogmatic in approach as the earlier novel.

Not everybody shared these opinions, however. There were people such as Marta Pessarrodona, a Catalan literary critic and writer herself, who gave a much more sympathetic vision of Lessing on that same page of *Diario 16* (p. 20). Pessarrodona referred to the success of *The Golden Notebook* in Europe, mentioning particularly the recent Prix Medici in France, and wrote about the intellectual and personal qualities she had discovered in Lessing when she interviewed her in Hampstead in January 1978; she goes further than the usual limits of criticism in a newspaper, as when she comments on the radical change Lessing was producing with her latest novel, *Shikasta* (its Spanish version was published *seven* years later, in 1986). Ana Antón-Pacheco, on the other hand, rejects Martín Gaite's attacks some months later in a review of the first three novels of the pentalogy for *El País* (1980). She defends Lessing on the grounds of her development in *Children of Violence* and draws particular attention to *The Four-Gated City* (not translated until 1982), where the abandonment of that naturalistic style so disapproved of by Martín Gaite is more evident.

From this time onwards the reception of Lessing in Spain has been in general wider and based on better knowledge, so that we can speak of a 'second period' of criticism. This is due perhaps to the social and cultural changes that the country experienced four or five years after Franco's death. The first years after the end of dictatorship – when *A Proper Marriage* and *The Golden Notebook* were translated and reviewed in the way we have seen above – were indeed characterised by an exciting and confusing atmosphere, when suddenly almost all that had been forbidden some years before was now allowed.

This is what made the 'revolutionary' Lessing of the fifties and early sixties so attractive for many people who felt deeply sympathetic towards the left and the radical movements. Although no real and independent feminist movement emerged at that time in Spain, because women were fighting beside men in the leftist political parties to achieve the liberties heretofore denied (a priority for many men and women in those years), Lessing's African novels and *The Golden Notebook* helped some women become conscious of their role in society and the struggle they must lead to enhance civil rights. This period (1975–80) was also a time of strikes, of great social restlessness, of the first democratic general election (1977) after four decades of dictatorship, of the elaboration of a democratic constitution (1978), of the return of many artists and politicians who were living in exile, of the final legalisation of the Communist Party (1977), of the advancement of the left in all institutions. For this reason, Lessing and her works are understandably seen as something formerly forbidden (communism, democracy, feminism . . .) that must be very quickly permitted, recovered and integrated in the social and cultural life of the country. Hence the simplification and distortion that most of Lessing's works suffer after the mid-sixties.

But a slight and progressive change in the reception of this author can be detected in some circles after about 1980; we see, for instance, that two interviews with the novelist by Nissa Torrents and Fernando Galván and Bernd Dietz (reprinted in the *Doris Lessing Newsletter*) were originally published in Spain in 1980 and 1983 respectively. Other testimonies of the eighties, some prior to Lessing's trip to Spain, are papers delivered at academic conferences, or essays published in academic journals, such as Pilar Hidalgo's studies on *Shikasta* in *Atlantis* (1981) and on *The Golden Notebook* in *Epos* (1984) or Linda Weinhouse's essay on *The Grass Is Singing* in *Revista Canaria de Estudios Ingleses* (1984) as well as Fernando Galván's book on the short stories (1982).

These are contributions from the Spanish universities, where Lessing is generally well known and appreciated. When she came to Spain in April 1983, the novelist confessed to Blanca Berasátegui in the conservative newspaper *ABC* that the young people at the universities were the ones who understood her novels better than the professional critics who 'are always insisting on classifying and pigeonholing those who write (Berasátegui, p. 42); and that is possibly why her brief tour in this country consisted of two lectures at the Universidad Autónoma in Madrid (on 19 April) and the Universidad Central in Barcelona (on 21 April) about the 'world of the novel', lectures that were followed by a session of questions and answers that confirmed the general confusion existing in Spain about her works.[3] Most of the articles published by the major newspapers during that week reflect this state of opinion, with the remarkable exceptions of the contributions of Ana Antón-Pacheco in *El País* (p. 38) and Aránzazu Usandizaga in *La Vanguardia* (p. 45), both professors of English at the Universities of Madrid and Barcelona, who offered excellent accounts of Lessing's career as a writer.

The rest of the papers gave very topical or superficial (when not openly distorted) information about the writer, reiterating that earlier cliché describing her as a lapsed feminist and communist that Lessing so deeply deplores; Gloria Díez in *Diario 16*, for example, insisting again that *The Golden Notebook* be seen exclusively from the perspective of the feminist question as well as in relation to Lessing's private life (her two marriages and love of gardening); and Fèlix Pujol in *La Vanguardia*, presenting Lessing as a feminist, asked her why she had abandoned her political convictions and told his readers that she had come to Spain to promote her latest work, *The Four-Gated City*!

The interest in Lessing after her tour of 1983 seems to decrease within literary circles until her second trip to Spain in March 1987, although *The Grass Is Singing* (for some critics still her best work) and *The Summer Before the Dark* were again translated in 1984, and *Briefing for a Descent into Hell* in 1985; other titles were reprinted: *The Golden Notebook* (1983, 1987), *The Memoirs of a Survivor* (1983), *The Habit of Loving* (1983) and *A Man and Two Women* (1984). The only absolute novelties in these four years have been the *Collected African Stories* in three volumes (1984, 1985 and 1987), the versions of *Shikasta* (1986), edited by a publisher of science fiction, and *Particularly Cats* (1986). The reviews of these books have been very few, mostly simple notices of their appearance. Certainly the publication of *Shikasta* has provoked no controversy among Spanish critics. María José Obiol, for example, after summarising the plot of the novel in *El País* sees it as a failure because the author has abandoned her forte, that is, the 'realistic' narration of the specific and the personal: 'This work by Lessing where the cosmic and the impersonal are blurred lacks the power of the writing that grows itself when speaking of the concrete and the personal' (p. 4).

Her visit to Madrid and Barcelona in March 1987 was reduced to some interviews with journalists in order to present the Catalan and Spanish translations of *The Good Terrorist*, which were extensively publicised, and although some mistakes were again produced in the press (*Shikasta* is described by Jorge Lech and Juan C. Insua in *La Vanguardia* as a 'trilogy'; and Francesc Arroyo writes for *El País* (1987a, p. 1) that *The Diary of a Good Neighbour* was published after *The Good Terrorist*; no mention is made of *If the Old Could . . .*), the general evaluation of her work was much more positive. The reviewer 'C.B.' of the Catalan newspaper *Avui* commented, for example, on the enthusiastic reception of the novel by Alison Lurie in the *New York Review of Books* and on the Jane Somers affair and Lessing's latest book *The Wind Blows Away Our Words* (p. 28). Other papers, such as *El País* or *La Vanguardia*, mentioned her work in progress, the opera adaptation of *The Making of the Representative for Planet 8*, and showed a real interest in avoiding the topical description of Lessing as a feminist or a former communist, which has prevailed until now, due perhaps – as has been suggested above – to the natural relevance of ideological and feminist questions in post-dictatorship Spain, when people were finally allowed to express their opinions freely. Now that political life in Spain is no longer centred on ideology, but has turned to the 'monotonous debates on economy' characteristic of Western democracies (so described by the Socialist Prime Minister González, when accused by the left of abandoning the old ideology of his party), the reception of Lessing seems (or promises at least) to be more genuine, and the case of *The Good Terrorist* may be symptomatic; the reviews of the translations into Catalan and Spanish have concentrated mostly on the theme of terrorism and the writer's vision of this problem.

An important reflection of the change that has been produced in the knowledge of the writer was the interesting and long interview that Pilar Trenas had with Lessing on the Spanish television programme 'Muy personal' (broadcast in April 1987), in which the novelist seemed to feel comfortable and talked amiably about her writing habits, rejected the vision of *Martha Quest* and other novels in the sequence of *Children of Violence* as autobiographical (she promised to write an autobiography before dying in order to prove it), commented on the 'historical' value of *The Golden Notebook* and on the purpose and effects of the novels of Jane Somers, and explained the necessity to write 'space-fiction' in *Canopus*. Moreover, she talked about the device of the 'dead language' used in *The Good Terrorist* to present the manipulation we suffer today in politics, religion, etc. It was on the whole an excellent introduction to the 'real' Lessing *par elle même*, who had, in this case, an interlocutor that knew exactly what they were talking about, something that cannot be said of the other interviewers during her 1983 trip.

Later in the year *The Diary of a Good Neighbour* was translated, although it did not have the same echo as in other countries (no indication is given that 'Jane Somers' is a pseudonym; the book is presented as 'another' novel by Lessing). The reception of *The Diary* seems to take us back some years, producing, as it does, curious mistakes and misunderstandings in spite of the general change in reception reflected above. *The Diary* seems an exception (and a defeat, if we consider Lessing's purpose in publishing it under a pseudonym). Some critics and reviewers have certainly dealt, in a somewhat superficial way, with the Somers 'affair', but they have done it – ironically – in an extraordinarily confusing manner, since none of the three references I have seen in the literary pages of the newspaper *El País* succeed in spelling the name of Lessing's *alter ego* correctly. In an interview with Lessing by the French writer François-Olivier Rousseau, printed in August 1985, Jane Somers appears as 'Janet Somers'; later, in March 1987 when Lessing visits Spain, Francesc Arroyo refers to *The Diary* as being signed with the pseudonym of 'Jane Sommers'; and finally when Constantino Bértolo reviews the translation of that novel in October 1987 he spells several times the name as 'Jean Somers'. That a name such as this is *never* properly spelt (in a paper with a good reputation) seems a proof of the confusion that still surrounds Lessing in this country. The conclusion can easily be drawn, a conclusion that is obviously far from being favourable to reviewers (have they really read the book they are writing about, and if so, why do they make so many mistakes of this sort?), that confirms Lessing's apprehensions about reviewers and critics.

On the other hand, the rest of the *Canopus* series has not been translated into Spanish (they seem to be considered 'subliterary' products of little value), and there are still other older works that remain ignored by Spanish readers, such as *Retreat to Innocence*, *Going Home* and all the plays; nevertheless, I believe that this 'second period' in Lessing criticism may be seen as a decisive change in the appreciation of the novelist that must be due not only to her two recent visits to Spain, but also (and mainly perhaps) to the new cultural atmosphere of the country that is today characterised by less ideological formulations than existed in the later seventies or early eighties; the clichés of the sixties and seventies have been abandoned, and now, in the late eighties, the Spanish common reader seems to be able to approach Lessing's work without the burden of labels such as 'Angry Young Woman', 'feminist', 'disappointed communist', etc. The chaotic chronology of the translations provokes curious mistakes, of course, but the general panorama seems to have changed substantially, and the proof is that critical studies of her work are now being published, such as the long chapter (sixty-five pages) dedicated to Lessing in a recent book by Pilar Hidalgo, *La crisis del realismo en la novela inglesa contemporánea*.

Lessing is not yet popular enough to be studied in high school or in the majority of Spanish universities, but the conditions for this to happen seem now, in 1988, much nearer than five years ago when she first visited the country and felt perhaps astounded at hearing discussed so many outdated topics as regards her work and herself. Some readers may still only know her as the author of *The Golden Notebook*, her most popular novel, and one that has been frequently reissued in new editions by several publishing houses. Probably for the younger generation of feminists she remains a writer who helps open their eyes to the world. It is important, however, to note that she is larger than her earlier reputation, and that some of her latest fiction is known and appreciated by large numbers of readers.

The ambivalent reception that Lessing has suffered in Spain is still present and despite the hopeful and optimistic conclusion of this article, the way ahead seems long and full of obstacles that are at the present time difficult to overcome. It is true that Lessing, for the Spanish reader and critic, is no longer the 'leftist' writer of earlier decades; but a structural problem still exists, that is, the chaotic state of the book industry in Spain and the lack of serious criteria exhibited by most publishers and reviewers. As a consequence, books that should be translated and reviewed immediately (as they are in other European countries) must suffer a long and strange delay. *The Fifth Child*, for example, has not even been mentioned in the press so far (September 1988).

But this situation is not germane to Lessing alone; far from being exceptional and unique, it has happened to other well-known writers such as Iris Murdoch or Muriel Spark, whose works have experienced a similar (and even worse) treatment. And while these conditions persist, the Spanish reader must feel isolated, receiving new European and American literary works years after they have appeared in other countries, and often accompanied by distorted secondhand information. A very recent case is, for instance, the translation of some fragments from John Haffenden's interview with Malcolm Bradbury (originally published in 1985 in *Novelists in Interview*) in *El País* (21 August 1988). It appeared *three years* later, and is presented with no reference whatever to the time when the interview took place; no mention is made either of Bradbury's 'recent' works, *Cuts* or *Mensonge*. The Spanish reader is thus led to believe that Bradbury's latest novel is *Rates of Exchange* (1983)! If we consider this, or the fact that 'young' writers of a certain reputation, such as Ian McEwan, Angela Carter or Fay Weldon, have not been translated into Spanish and are thus virtually unknown here, then what is happening with Lessing's *Canopus*, the *Diaries* and *The Fifth Child* does not seem so terrible; the ignorance of these works certainly provides evidence of a book-market and a cultural life that are not working as they should, but it is only one piece of evidence among many others, and probably not the worst.

Notes

1. For details on the translations and criticism mentioned in this paper, see Galván Reula (1987).
2. Although this interview, which is accompanied by brief bibliographical information, is one of the best and most interesting pieces published in Spain about Lessing, the confusion looms up again when the Spanish versions are mentioned: in 1980 *Children of Violence* is described as a tetralogy (cf. *La Calle* 106 (1–7 April 1980): 44).
3. Pilar Hidalgo mentions these confusions (1984, p. 97, n. 15).

Works Cited

Antón-Pacheco, Ana. 'Los años de aprendizaje de Doris Lessing'. *El País* (Literary Supplement) 18 May 1980: 4.
——. 'Doris Lessing, "cronista" de la mujer occidental'. *El País* 17 April 1983: 38.
Arroyo, Francesc. 'Terrorismo y literatura'. *El País* (Literary Supplement) 5 March 1987a: 1, 4.
——. 'Entre la comedia y el pavor'. *El País* (Literary Supplement) 5 March 1987b: 4.
Berasátegui, Blanca. 'Doris Lessing: "Los universitarios son quienes mejor entienden mis novelas"'. *ABC* 19 April 1983: 47.
Bértolo, Constantino. 'Crisis a medida'. *El País* (Literary Supplement) 29 October 1987: 2.
Blanch, Antonio. 'Un casamiento convencional'. *Reseña de literatura, arte y espectáculos* 123 (November–December 1979): 123/5–123/7.
'C.B.' 'Doris Lessing escriu una òpera'. *Avui* 11 March 1987: 28.
Díez, Gloria. 'Encuentros con . . . Doris Lessing'. *Diario 16* ('*Disidencias*', Cultural Supplement no. 123) 24 April 1983: iv–v.
Fernaud, Pedro. 'Hija de la violencia'. *Triunfo* 874 (27 October 1979): 54.
Galván Reula, Fernando. *Estudio lingüístico de las 'short stories' de Doris Lessing.* Secretariado de Publicaciones de la Universidad de La Laguna, 1982.
——. 'A Spanish Checklist of Translations and Criticism'. *Doris Lessing Newsletter* 11.1 (Spring 1987): 10–11, 15.
——. and Bernd Dietz. 'A Conversation with Doris Lessing'. *Revista Canaria de Estudios Ingleses* 6 (April 1983): 89–94. Reprinted in *Doris Lessing Newsletter* 9.1 (1985): 5–13.
Haffenden, John. 'Malcolm Bradbury: "Todo arte es fraude"'. *El País* 21 August 1988: 20.
Hidalgo, Pilar. 'La crisis del realismo en Doris Lessing: *Shakasta*'. *Atlantis* 3.1 (1981): 103–10.
——. 'Cambio histórico y forma narrativa en *The Golden Notebook* de Doris Lessing'. *Epos* (Revista de Filologia, UNED) i (1984): 85–101.
——. *La crisis del realismo en la novela inglesa Contemporánea.* Servicio de Publicaciones de la Universidad de Málaga, 1987.
Lech, Jorge and Juan C. Insua. [Interview with Doris Lessing]. *La Vanguardia* 10 March 1987: p. 46.

Martín Gaite, Carmen. 'Los peligros del dogmatismo'. *Diario 16* 12 November 1979: 20.

Obiol, Maria José. 'Universo cósmico'. *El País* (Literary Supplement) 24 July 1986: 4.

Pérez Gállego, Cándido. *Literatura y rebeldía en la Inglaterra actual*. Madrid: CSIC, 1968. 55, 102–14.

Pérez Minik, Domingo. *Introducción a la novela inglesa actual*. Madrid: Guadarrama, 1968. 246–51.

——. *La novela extranjera en España*. Madrid: Taller de Ediciones Josefina Betancor, 1973. 179–86.

——. ' "Un casamiento convencional" de Doris Lessing'. *Insula* 400–1 (March–April 1980): 29.

Pessarrodona, Marta. 'Doris Lessing, de cerca'. *Diario 16* (12 November 1979): 20.

Pujol, Félix. 'Entrevista con Doris Lessing'. *La Vanguardia* 22 April 1983: 25.

Rousseau, François-Olivier. 'Más allá de la literatura. Doris Lessing: "El libro sólo ya no basta",' *El País* (Literary Supplement) 11 August 1985: 1–3.

Torrents, Nissa. 'Doris Lessing. Del testimonio al misticismo'. *La Calle* 106 (1–7 April 1980): 42–4. Reprinted in *Doris Lessing Newsletter* (Winter 1980).

Torres, Maruja. 'La autora de "El cuaderno dorado" y "Los hijos de la violencia" habla en España de su obra'. *El País* 19 April 1983: 30.

Usandizaga, Aránzazu. 'Doris Lessing y los cataclismos que Vivimos'. *La Vanguardia* 26 April 1983: 45.

Weinhouse, Linda. 'Incest and Repression in Doris Lessing's *The Grass Is Singing*'. *Revista Canaria de Estudios Ingleses* 8 (April 1984): 99–117.

9

A Case of Chronic Anachronisms: Doris Lessing and the USSR

LORNA M. PETERSON

Why has the white man dreamed so fabulous a dream of freedom and human dignity and again and again tried to kill his own dream?   (Lillian Smith, Foreword to *Killers of the Dream*)

No other nation, with the exception of those countries in which she has lived – Persia, Southern Rhodesia, England – has been as prominent in the writings of Doris Lessing as has the Soviet Union. The first home of communism, the leader of the socialist world, the betrayer of leftist ideals, the invader of Afghanistan, these are some of the roles the USSR has played in Lessing's life and work. If Lessing's attitude toward the Soviet Union has changed dramatically over time so, too, has the official Soviet view of Lessing. In fact, the degree of change – hers and theirs – only confirms Lessing's own conviction that ideology and dogma are short-lived. Her judgement of the Soviet Union and the Soviet judgement on Lessing tend always to be somewhat faulty, out of sync, anachronistic.

In the Soviet Union to date there are only two Lessings; crudely put, the Southern African anti-racist, progressive peace activist of the fifties, and the English, conservative mystic of the seventies and eighties. The Lessing of the sixties hardly exists. Given what we know of pre-Gorbachev Russia it is not surprising to find literary classifications that fit so tightly the political glove of the Soviet Communist Party. The degree to which this is true, however, is unsettling. As unsettling as is the vehemence with which Lessing now condemns the Soviet state as 'the most brutal, cynical regime of its time' (*Wind*, p. 166).

Lessing's introduction to this 'brutal' regime, it turns out, came long before her well-known trip there in 1952 as part of a delegation of English writers. In a recent autobiographical piece, Lessing recalls a childhood journey across the Soviet Union from the Caspian Sea to Moscow, a trip no other Western family had yet ventured. Her parents, with two small children in tow, were making their way back from Persia to England. The brutality of the Soviet Union at that time, 1924, lay mostly in its poverty and defencelessness. The revolutionary Bolshevik regime, still experimenting in economic as well as aesthetic principles under the New Economic Policy (NEP), was no challenge for Maude Tayler, Lessing's mother. Lessing's first memory of the Soviet Union is informed by a family legend, frequently and amusedly repeated by her father, of the way in which her mother talked, indeed bullied, the four into the Soviet Union. The vision she conjures up from her childhood is of a 'poor ragged half-starved Bolshevik with a rifle "that wouldn't bring down a pigeon," confronted by a British matron' (*Granta*, p. 63).

As a young woman coming of age in Southern Rhodesia, she had imagined a nation of communists believing in justice for all barring none, including blacks. It was not until 1952 that the adult Lessing, now resident in England, a published writer strongly indebted to the great Russian realists, and a communist, again visited there. This trip, too, would have a lasting impact. In writing about that trip, in 'The Small Personal Voice' and in the preface to the *African Stories*, Lessing talks of her mistrust of socialist realism, her doubts about an aesthetic view and a political system that subjugates the individual, especially the artist, to the collective:

What is dangerous is the inner loyalty to something felt as something much greater than one's self. I remember, in Moscow, when this question was discussed, a writer replied to an accusation of being bludgeoned by the Party into false writing by saying: 'No one bludgeons us. Our conscience is at the service of the people. We develop an inner censor.' It is the inner censor which is the enemy.   (*Voice*, p. 12)

This sums up for me, and where I feel it most deeply and personally, the point where 'committedness' can sell out to expediency. Once you admit that 'art should be willing to stand aside for life,' then the little tracts about progress, the false optimism, the dreadful lifeless products of socialist realism, become inevitable.   (*Voice*, p. 13)

Lessing's own experiment with socialist realism, 'Hunger', she declared a failure (*African Stories*, p. ix). She consciously tried, as a result of her discussions with writers in the Soviet Union, to create the kind of story in which there is clear-cut good and bad. If Dickens could do it so successfully in novel after novel about nineteenth-century industrial England, she argued, then surely it was possible to do so using twentieth-century colonial Africa. Although a failure to the author, in the Soviet Union 'Hunger' became one of the most translated, anthologised and positively reviewed of her works.

The Soviet translations and reviews are not many, however.[1] In the fifties they consisted almost entirely of a few of the African stories, excerpts from *Going Home* and *Martha Quest*. Not surprisingly, the writer the Soviet establishment wanted readers to know was the one who, primarily in short stories and novellas, wrote disparagingly of white colonialism in Southern Africa and sympathetically of the black population. She is invariably described at this time as 'a prominent English writer and social activist' (Lessing, *Kom. Pravda*, p. 4, and Ivanov) which was true.

Novyi Mir, one of the most respected Russian literary journals, published a translation of 'The Old Chief Mshlanga' as early as 1953. In a very brief biographical sketch and introduction to Lessing, we have the gist of how she was to be received and presented in the Soviet Union during the rest of the decade:

Doris Lessing (born in 1919) progressive English writer, author of two novels and a collection of novellas. She spent her childhood and youth in Southern Rhodesia (Southeast Africa). After finishing college [*sic*] she worked for the telephone company, in offices, etc. In 1950, she published her first novel – *The Grass Is Singing*, which brought attention to the young writer. One of the basic themes of her work is the cultural life of the Negro population of Southern Rhodesia under the oppression of the white colonialists. Nowadays D. Lessing lives in England, participates in the movement for world peace, works for progressive publications. Last year, together with a group of English writers she visited the Soviet Union. (Lessing, *Novyi Myr*, p. 180)[2]

After her visit to the Soviet Union, several stories and collections of stories were published, 'Hunger' and 'The Antheap' being the most frequently translated. Both also appeared under the title *No Witchcraft for Sale*, in a 1956 edition of seven stories in English, published in Moscow. (The others, in addition to the title story, are 'The Old Chief Mshlanga', 'The Nuisance', 'Little Tembi', '"Leopard" George'.) The collection includes a preface by A. P. Sarukhanyan and commentary by G. G. Yudinoy (see Nagurski-Bernstein). The commentary is mostly aimed at students of English who will be reading the stories. The preface is far more interesting; it establishes the official attitude on Lessing for potential readers of her works in the original English.

Sarukhanyan repeats the then accepted Soviet wisdom on Lessing: 'Doris Lessing stands in the front ranks of the English workers' movement. Together with the best representatives of contemporary progressive English literature she is active in the enlightened work of the World Defence League of English Writers' (Sarukhanyan, p. iii). In what is one of the longest commentaries (thirteen pages) in Russian on Lessing's work, Sarukhanyan's preface emphasises over and over again the concern in the stories with the people, the African people, and with the oppression of British colonialism. There is an internal unity to all the stories, according to Sarukhanyan, and that unity is 'the theme of the people, of the rightful masters of their own country, whom the English colonialists have conquered by deception and force' (p. iv). Only one year later, in 'The Small Personal Voice', Lessing would disavow such unimaginative approaches to art and describe the literature of the socialist world as 'intolerably dull and false . . . one reads it yawning and returns to Tolstoy' (*Voice*, p. 11).

Although he doesn't abandon his central point on what is Lessing's central point, Sarukhanyan is somewhat more interesting in his discussion of the individual stories. He notices, but does not elaborate on, Lessing's exploration into the dehumanisation of the ruling, white society. Brutal and barbaric in its treatment of the African, colonialism turns its rulers into beasts. Even those who would be kind cannot be. The system, as in 'Little Tembi', makes a mockery of philanthropy and individual acts of conscience; its corruptive influence goes beyond hypocrisy, corroding the moral fibre of the white man.

Lessing's African stories are as much about the psychic damage done to the white society as about the outrages committed against blacks. In this she is reminiscent of the Southern American writer, Lillian Smith (1897–1966), who was one of the first white Southerners to attack racism and in doing so point to the profound harm it does to the white person. In *Killers of the Dream* (1949), Smith, like Lessing, writes of the strange double-think of those who would be good Christians and good racists simultaneously; 'to be' as Smith states it, 'a gentlewoman and an arrogant callous creature in the same moment; to pray at night and ride a Jim Crow car the next morning and to feel comfortable doing both' (*Killers*, p. 20). Lessing similarly wonders at the capacity of the white settler to be both a kind, good Christian and a cruel, inhumane master, never seeing the inconsistency.[3] Unfortunately, Soviet criticism of Lessing's African stories only hints at this dimension. The reviewers are far more focused on the African as he appears, or as they construe him to appear. Sarukhanyan again: 'in Doris Lessing's stories blacks are drawn as people who are inquisitive, gifted, independent, freedom-loving, proud, truly humane, able to create things of great material and cultural value' (p. vi).

Five Stories, the first collection of her works in Russian, was published in 1955, two years after it appeared in Great Britain under the title *Five*. A review in *Literaturnaya Gazeta*, announcing the publication of *Five Stories*, once again described Lessing to the Russian reader as a 'progressive'. She is complimented particularly for introducing in 'Hunger' the progressive element of the African people in the characters Samu and Mizi. 'The collection, *Five Stories'*, the reviewer concludes, 'is an interesting and truthful book. You feel it, like the warm handshake of the author herself' (Golovnya).

Lessing later, in *The Golden Notebook*, would mock such judgements. Pinned to the black notebook are reviews of *Frontiers of War* which Anna Wulf has cut from various Soviet publications:

Terrible indeed is the exploitation in British colonies revealed in this courageous first novel, written and published under the very eye of the oppressor to reveal to the world the real truth behind British imperialism   (p. 443)

we look at her work with an eager expectation which is not justified. Yet let us welcome what she has given, looking forward with hope to what she might, indeed will, give us, when she comes to understand that a true artistic work must have a revolutionary life.   (p. 444)

She is the only representative of the people in this book, and yet her character remains shadowy, undeveloped, unsatisfying. No, the author must learn from our literature, the literature of health and progress, that no one is benefited by despair. This is a negative novel. We detect Freudian influences.   (p. 445)

Compare these to excerpts from actual Soviet commentaries:

Her colourful descriptions remind us of the romantics, and the interest in psychological problems, in combination with a sober realism, of the classic English and Russian novel. But this does not prevent Lessing's stories from also being contemporary: they are addressed to what concerns the millions. More than that, the devotion of the author to the humanistic tradition truly strengthens the resonance of her book.   (Landor, p. 252)

From the sickly psychologism, characteristic of her first novel, *The Grass Is Singing*, she has moved in her last productions toward constructions of realistic, psychologically profound forms. The tradition of bourgeois psychologism is not always easy for this writer to overcome, but she steadfastly seeks new themes and new heroes, and her particular failures do not destroy the overall path of her development.   (Sarukhanyan, p. xv).

Her first novel, *The Grass Is Singing* (1950), is yet penetrated by the spirit of sickly psychologism.   (*Istoriya*, p. 719).

The comparison forces us to agree with Lessing that 'something has happened in the world which has made parody impossible' (*GN*, p. 440).[4]

One of those things, perhaps, was socialist realism. Soviet reviewers of the fifties found little to criticise in 'Hunger', Lessing's only attempt at creating a socialist realist tale. They praised in it precisely what Lessing deemed its failure, and declared it a moral victory. Jabavu has a choice between the reality of the white man's city and the dreams of an African community. That he ultimately sees the light and finds the true road, the road to an awakened 'black' Africa, is a good. He has chosen between the lies that are colonial Africa and the socialist truth that will be – an enlightened Africa belonging to Africans. He has rejected the self, the 'I' for the community, the 'we', the collective.

It is hard to argue with either Lessing or the Soviets. As a story it fails; as a socialist realist fable it succeeds. But these are limited judgements. The Soviet judgement is just one more 'label' of the many, from East and West, Lessing has rejected over the years. Hers is more interesting. Why is 'Hunger' a failure? Her attempt to write, as Dickens did, 'a story of simple good and bad, with clear-cut choices' (*African Stories*, p. ix) doesn't come off because Lessing, even then, was unconvinced of simple 'either/or' choices. 'Hunger' is most interesting and most successful when it presents, as it frequently does, complex, multiple and simultaneous 'truths', the 'and, and, and' as Charles Watkins would say.

Jabavu's mother, for example, recalls a very different past than does her husband. For him life is simple; it either is good and from the pre-colonial past or bad and part of the British present. The father says: 'Every person knew what it was they should do and how that thing should be done. . . We knew, then, what was good and what was evil.' The mother thinks, but does not say: 'he longs so much for the old times, which he understood, that he has forgotten how one tribe harried another, he has forgotten that in this part of the country we lived in terror because of the tribes from the South' (*Five*, p. 265). The mother, like the author, knows that nothing is as simple as her husband would have it.

The good guys, Mr Samu and Mr Mizi, and the bad guys, Jerry and the gang, are flat. They do not have the flair, the eccentricity, the absurdity of Dickens characters. The good ones have no colour, no language but the deadly, stultifying vocabulary of a socialist pamphlet: 'trade union, organisation, politics, committee, reaction, progress, society, patience, education' (*Five*, p. 285). Among the bad ones Jerry is no Fagin, Betty no Nancy, and certainly the gang cannot boast of anyone like the Artful Doger. Of course, Jabavu isn't Oliver Twist either. Jabavu courts his own destiny, resembling more a positive hero of socialist realism than a Dickens ingenu.

The story fails largely because its ending doesn't work. The reader simply cannot believe in the sudden victory of the 'men of light', the total acceptance by Jabavu of the collective, the exchange of the 'I' for the 'we' the Soviet critics were so fond of extolling. What those critics fail to recognise is that Jabavu's conversion to socialism is no more convincing than Raskolnikov's to Christ at the end of *Crime and Punishment*. For one thing, neither character has been shown to have the humility such conversions require.

The Soviets like 'The Antheap' as much as 'Hunger'. In the

fifties, the story was published in a number of journals, anthologised several times and issued in a separate edition of 150,000 copies. Not surprisingly, they tend to see 'The Antheap' solely as a moral tale of how two youngsters bravely and successfully fight the colour bar:

> The story tells of how the good and true friendship of the boys widens their horizon. Dirk, with help from his friend, quickly gets through the school programme. Tommy, also thanks to this friendship, learns to understand life around him, to look at it with the eyes of the oppressed masses.   (Sarukhanyan, p. xii).

> Doris Lessing draws a touching and tender friendship, boyish in its restraint.   (Sarukhanyan, p. xiii).

For Sarukhanyan, it represented Lessing's move (literally, since the story ends with the boys about to go to the city to study) in the later African stories toward 'realism', which would eventually lead her to the city, the African workers and the story of Jabavu.

Soviet propaganda was to be served by Lessing even better than through her fiction when, in 1956, she went home to Southern Rhodesia. Her trip she tells us, eleven years after the fact, was paid in large part by the Soviet Union. Seeking financial backing from the British press failed, so 'With my departure date a month off, on an impulse, I got onto a bus to Fleet Street, walked into Tass and proposed to a charming but surprised young man behind a desk that Tass should pay for my fare home. Every civilised country in the world, said I, paid journalists to visit countries and report on what they found there, and why should not Russia do the same?' (*Going Home*, p. 314). Her mother could not have executed the scene better. Lessing attributes her own success to 'the usefulness of naivete'. If so, it is very much the same combination of naivete and a righteous, British sense of what is civilised that got her family across the Soviet Union years earlier.

The Soviets did, in fact, publish her articles; excerpts, at least, appeared in both *Literaturnaya Gazeta* and *Komsomolskaya Pravda*. Starting on 28 June and ending on 13 September 1956, *Literaturnaya Gazeta* published a series of six extended articles from *Going Home*, entitled 'Toward the South From Sahara' ('K Yugu ot Sakhari'). The series was introduced with a very brief commentary on Lessing and the articles to follow, mentioning merely that Lessing, a member of the World Defence League of English Writers, author of *The Grass Is Singing* and short stories, had lived in Southern Rhodesia for twenty-five years and had just returned from a visit there that spring. The original drawings by Paul Hogarth were published along with the correspondence.

In 'Eleven Years Later', the afterword to the 1967 edition of *Going Home*, Lessing complained of the major editing job, with cuts and bits added, the Russians performed on her articles. 'Now comes the real unforgiveable naivete. It never occurred to me, since the conditions I was describing were so black a case against "imperialism" they could not be worse, that there was any need at all for them to gild their lily' (p. 316). Gild would seem the wrong word; what the Soviets did was strip the articles of almost all allusions which did not directly deal with racism, including many of Lessing's finest descriptions of Africa, most interesting observations and most moving reminiscences. Of course the problem is that we do not know exactly what the Russians expunged from her correspondence and what she later added when the articles were converted to a book.

Komsomolskaya Pravda printed one excerpt from *Going Home* which appeard on 11 October 1956. It was introduced by two brief articles on Lessing. The first, entitled 'The Persecution of the Writer Doris Lessing' ('Presledovanie Pisatel'nitsi Doris Lessing'), is a brief Tass report on Lessing's having been prohibited entry into the Federation of Central Africa (the ill-fated union of Nyasaland, Northern and Southern Rhodesia) and the Union of South Africa. She is quoted as saying there were two reasons for this: one, her communism; two, her attitude against racism. Somewhat late in its newsworthiness, this report was published in the 5 October issue.

Four days later, another article on Lessing, accompanied by her photograph, was published. Bearing the title 'Return to the Homeland' ('Vozvrashchenie na Rodinu'), it was meant to introduce the reader to Lessing and provide some background to the forthcoming excerpt from *Going Home*. The excerpt from the book appeared on 11 October. It deals with Lessing's reminiscence of an event in 1947: the disappearance of a servant, Dickson, caught up in the political agitation surrounding the first big strike in Southern Rhodesia. A tale like this, of strikes and racial killings, of workers and industrial Africa was bound to appeal more to the

Soviets than an idyll of the African landscape, however politically correct it may have seemed.

Lessing's stories continued to appear occasionally in Soviet periodicals during the remainder of the fifties. A translation of *Martha Quest* was published in 1957. Then there is almost a complete blackout on Lessing during the sixties.[5] In the early part of the decade a few stories were published in other languages of the Soviet Union and in 1964 *Nash Sovremennik* published 'The Other Woman' ('Drugaya Zhenshchina'). The entry on Lessing in the 1970 edition of the *Great Soviet Encyclopedia*, after mentioning her African stories and anti-colonialist writings, states: 'In the mid-fifties Lessing lived through an ideological crisis, best described in the novel, *The Golden Notebook* (1962). The play, *Play With a Tiger*[6] (1962), and the collection of stories, *A Man and Two Women* (1963), treats the theme of the despair of contemporary stoicism.'

Very little of Lessing appeared in the 1970s. Curiously, however, the Soviets did translate *The Summer Before the Dark*, which was published in the journal *Foreign Literature* (*Inostrannaya Literatura*), in 1977. In 1976, *Nedel'ya* (the weekly supplement of *Izvestiya*, the daily organ of the Soviet government) also republished 'The Antheap', but under a new title, 'Two Boys', and in an abridged version. It was to be published yet again in *Oktyabr'*, in 1984.

In 1980, in honour of the new, independent republic of Zimbabwe, *The Grass Is Singing* was finally published in the Soviet Union. It appeared in the 5 May and 6 June issues of *Oktyabr'* with a two-page introduction by the political reviewer for Tass, Sergei Kulik. No mention is made of the psychological dimensions of the novel. It is presented simply as an anti-racist tract about 'the beginning of the end of "white" Africa': 'The passive protest of the "niggers" read by D. Lessing's whites in the eyes of their servants, developed into a triumphant war of liberation.' The reader is reminded that Lessing, the 'progressive writer' (truly an anachronism in 1980), is also the author of such works as *Martha Quest*, *The Summer Before the Dark*, 'The Old Chief Mshlanga' and 'The Antheap' (*Oktyabr'*, 5 May 1980, p. 145).

The only other translation in the early eighties was 'The Old Lady and a Cat', which appeared in *Literary Russia* (*Literaturnaya Rossiya*) in 1981. Given the graphic description in the story of the poverty visited upon the elderly in capitalist Britain, it is not surprising that of all the later, post-African stories this one would be chosen. For the Soviets, this is the old Lessing, the fellow-traveller concerned for humanity, critical of the social, political and economic realities of the West. This is the Lessing the Soviet reader had always known.

And then a curious thing happened. An open, impassioned attack on Lessing was published in the 11 May 1983 issue of *Literaturnaya Gazeta*. The article, 'Women and War: The "Comforting" Reasoning of Doris Lessing under the Shadow of the Nuclear Threat' (Vasil'eva) is not based on any particular work of Lessing's. In fact, the provocation for the attack appears to have been the interview article, 'Doris Lessing on Feminism, Communism, and "Space Fiction"' by Lesley Hazleton, published the previous summer in the *New York Times Magazine* (1982). Hazleton and the *New York Times* are never mentioned, however, even though whole phrases are lifted from the *Times'* pages.

The Russian article begins with the words 'Yaroslavna cries early (in the morning)' ('Yaroslavna rano plachet'), an evocation of the refrain from Yaroslavna's lament in the old Russian epic, 'The Song of Igor's Campaign'. Assumed to be a twelfth-century document, the epic has a strong claim on the Russian imagination. Its lament for those who lay dead in battle reverberates with memories of the Second World War and the enormous number of Russian casualities. Lessing is clearly going to be attacked for her disaffection with the peace movement and her more recent concern for survivalism.

Vasil'eva, the author of the article, laments the Lessing who was and harshly condemns the present-day Lessing, now seen as a tool of the capitalist system under which she lives. By disaffiliating herself from the peace movement and allowing herself to imagine the possibility of nuclear war, Lessing is accused of spreading Reagan's propaganda, of endorsing the Amercian president's insistence on continuing the arms race. Lessing's views on the coming ice age and the need for survival, her call to separate civil defence from the peace movement, are all lifted directly from the Hazleton interview.

One of Vasil'eva's major points is that Lessing's political philosophy is very important, that Lessing is not just any woman or any writer. Her voice echoes throughout the West. The following citation in English is from the Hazleton article, the Russian from Vasil'eva; it is almost a verbatim translation – as is much of the Russian article:

Doris Lessing is the kind of writer who has followers, not just readers. They have been committed to her largely because of her commitment to major issues, such as politics and feminism. Over the course of a distinguished 30-year writing career, she has led them into several very different worlds.   (p. 21).

Lessing – pisatel'nitsa, u kotoroi est' ne prosto chitateli i pochitateli. U neyo mnogo posledovatelei. Oni predany ei – v osnobnom iz-za eyo priverzhennosti k bol'shim problemam: politike i feminizmu. Na protyazhenii svoego tridtsatiletnego pisatel'skogo puti ona vela lyudei za soboyu razlichnye miry.   (p. 4)

The only difference between the English and the Russian is that in the Russian the word 'distinguished' is omitted from the description of Lessing's writing career.

Interestingly, reference to Lessing's former affiliation with communism is not ignored. It is both mentioned and commented upon . . . and in Vasil'eva's own words:

At one time she was taken with communist ideas, but Lessing did not go far: she wanted to see communism cloaked in sacred white garments, not having to stand up against evil; she did not want to think about how this new idea of humanity existed in hostile surroundings and could not go undefended. She did not want to see socialism in a realistic incarnation, and that is a pity, for Doris Lessing is not one of those who can be deceived by the high standard of living in England and America – she knows well and precisely the underside of her world.   (p. 4)

Lessing, the article concludes, didn't make it as a communist and doesn't make it as a contemporary woman. Since the Second World War, women all over the world have fought against war and for peace. And if (as Lessing claims in the Hazleton interview) in the forty years since the end of the war we have lived in relative peace, that great service is attributable to 'the little woman – the mother of mankind, joining a crowd of many millions doing battle for peace in the squares and on the streets of the cities saying "No more war"' (p. 4). These are the strong ones, the article concludes, and Doris Lessing, caught in her own despair, is a weak spirit.

A recent 1987 survey of British writing, *Angliiskaya Literatura: 1945–1980* does not vilify Lessing, but does not accord her much attention either. Under the general editorship of Sarukhanyan, the volume is divided into two time-periods – 1945 to the mid-sixties, the mid-sixties to 1980 – and each into three genres – prose, drama and poetry. Lessing is mentioned in the two prose sections and in the earlier section on drama. She is not, however, given a separate heading, as are such writers as Evelyn Waugh, C. P. Snow, Graham Greene, Lawrence Durrell, Anthony Powell, William Golding and John Osborne in the earlier period, and Angus Wilson, Iris Murdoch, John Fowles, Muriel Spark and James Aldrich in the later one. Instead, Lessing is folded into the general history of post-Second-World-War British literature. She is credited with being a short-story writer as well as a novelist, but the African stories, those the Soviet reader is most likely to recognise, are not even mentioned. Her interest in Sufism is seen as a trend among British writers of the time who, disillusioned with the crisis in bourgeois thought, are looking to the wisdom of Eastern religions and philosophies (*Ang. Lit.*, p. 29). Because of the *Children of Violence* series, she is also linked with Joyce Cary, Pamela Hansford Johnson, Evelyn Waugh, Jack Lindsey, J. R. R. Tolkien and Lawrence Durrell, who in the forties began the trend of writing novel-cycles (p. 40). In the later period, she is identified along with Margaret Drabble, Fay Weldon and Penelope Mortimer as writers of feminist prose (p. 254). Her short stories, like theirs, are said to have as a standing theme 'the fate, in large part unhappy, of contemporary woman' (p. 269).

Lessing's novels of the seventies – *Briefing for a Descent into Hell, The Summer Before the Dark, Memoirs of a Survivor* – are described as 'already showing the enthusiasm of the author for allegory, symbol, and parable' that will lead her to the series of 'cosmic' novels (p. 248). *Shikasta*, the only one of the *Canopus in Argos* series published before 1980, is briefly mentioned and its obvious allusion to the contemporary world is made explicit (p. 249). The longest reference in the entire volume to any one of Lessing's works is the discussion of the play, *Each His Own Wilderness*, discussed in the drama section as part of the 'Angry Young Men' of British literature. After a relatively lengthy synopsis of the play, the author (the sections on drama were written by M. M. Koreneva) concludes: 'The trouble is not that the sum total of the play results in bourgeois happiness, but that it might really be preferred to the variant of radicalism juxtaposed to it in the play' (p. 183).

Once again, the former communist has disappointed the Soviet reviewer. Given what has been translated from and written about Lessing, the typical Soviet reader, for whom the original English texts are not accessible, is probably confused. (But, then again, many of her readers in the West, with far more available to them, claim to be confused, too.) The important thing to remember is that the view of Lessing for the majority of Soviets is based on what appears in the official press. Since Soviet readers were introduced to her as a fellow-traveller, a friend of the Soviet Union, a fighter for social justice in the best Marxist-Leninist manner, she is unlikely to have developed an early following among dissidents. That some of her novels and stories may have been passed among those who read the unofficial *samizdat* press is possible, but hard to ascertain and unlikely. One imagines the Lessing now so critical of the Soviet Union could have strong support among the more unreconcilable dissidents . . . if they knew of her change of heart.

At present, Lessing seems to hold as hard a line against the Soviet Union as do those dissidents. If not before, then certainly today, in 1989, her unyielding condemnation appears incongruous, odd, another anachronism. Daily we receive reports from Moscow and Leningrad of what *glasnost* means. Voices once prominent in literature and politics, long dead to the Russian people, are being heard again, including the poet, Osip Mandel'stam, whose words 'and only my own kind will kill me' haunt Lessing at the end of *The Wind Blows Away Our Words* (p. 171).

Yet perhaps Lessing is not as intransigent as some would have it. Her greatest fiction has always allowed for change, dramatic change, and certainly she has been undaunted by the necessity of changing her own opinions. In a 1984 interview in *New Age Journal*, while talking about the similarities between communism and religion, Lessing said: 'What is interesting about Communism is that it started off as an extremely idealistic utopian dream; we know what it's turned into, so let's not go into that. But we know that tyrannies tend to soften as time goes on, or they fall apart and disappear' (Wilson, p. 89). She repeated these sentiments again in the 1985 Massey lectures later published as *Prisons We Choose to Live Inside*. In those lectures Gorbachev is given a parenthetical nod: '(The new ruler Gorbachev is trying to remedy this.)' 'This' is the ossification of Soviet thought (p. 72).

Current events would indicate that Lessing's parenthetical remark may have to expand into a full reassessment. If *glasnost* continues to invite more and more voices to be heard in the Soviet

Union, then Lessing and the Soviets will once again have to change their assessments of each other. Should that happen, this essay, too, will have become an anachronism.

Notes

1. I am deeply indebted to I. Babyonysheva of Moscow for her very generous help in finding works on and by Lessing in Russia; to the staffs of the Robert Frost Library, Amherst College and the Slavic and East European Library at the University of Illinois for their help in locating those works; and to Dale E. Peterson for his help in fetching and translating them.
2. All translations from the Russian are mine (LMP).
3. The comparison between Smith and Lessing goes even deeper and would make an interesting paper itself. Both authors, for instance, understood the dark dynamic, including the sexual politics, hidden in the silences required by a racist society.
4. For a full and extremely provocative discussion of parody in Lessing see James F. English's paper on 'Ideology as Pastiche' (1987).
5. Bibliographic searches here and investigations in the Soviet Union indicate that *The Golden Notebook* is yet to be translated.
6. The title is translated as a verb, *Play With a Tiger! (Igrai s tigrom)*. Russian is unable to contain in a single word the double-meaning possible in the English 'play'.

Works Cited

Angliiskaya Literatura: 1945–1980. Ed. A. P. Sarukhanyan. Moscow: Nauka, 1987.

Bol'shaya Sovetskaya Entsiklopediya. Vol. 4. Moscow, 1970. 1122–3.

English, James F. 'Ideology as Pastiche: Politics of the Postmodern in *The Golden Notebook*'. Unpublished paper presented at MLA, San Francisco, December 1987.

Golovnya, Irina. 'Pyat: Povestei Doris Lessing'. *Literaturnaya Gazeta* 22 November 1955: 4.

Hazleton, Lesley. 'Doris Lessing on Feminism, Communism, and "Space Fiction"'. *New York Times Magazine* 25 July 1982: 21ff.

Istoriya Angliiskoi Literatury. Tom III. Moscow: Akademiya Nauk SSSR, 1958: 719–20.

Ivanov, B. 'Doris Lessing: Vozvrashchenie na Rodinu'. *Komsomolskaya Pravda* 10 (9 October 1956): 4.

Landor, M. 'Kontrasti i Kharaktery Yuzhnoi Afriki'. *Druzhba Narodov* 6 (1959): 252–3.

Lessing, Doris. 'Staryi Vozhd Mshlanga'. Tr. Yu. Mirskaya. *Novyi Mir* 12 (1953): 180–8.

——. 'K Yugu ot Sakhari'. *Literaturnaya Gazeta* 28, 30 June; 7, 14, 28 July; 13 September 1956: 4.

——. 'Vozrashchenie na Rodinu'. *Komsomolskaya Pravda* 10 (11 October 1956): 4.

——. *African Stories*. New York: Fawcett, 1965.

——. *Going Home*. Herts: Panther, 1968.

——. *The Golden Notebook*. New York: Ballantine, 1968.

——. *Five*. Herts: Panther, 1969.

——. *A Small Personal Voice*. Ed. Paul Schlueter. New York: Vintage, 1975.

——. *Trava Poet*. Tr. A. Sergeeva. *Oktyabr'* 5 (1980): 5 May, 145–91; 6 June, 130–80.

——. 'Impertinent Daughters'. *Granta* 14 (Winter, 1984): 51–69.

——. *Prisons We Choose to Live Inside*. New York: Harper & Row, 1987.

——. *The Wind Blows Away Our Words*. New York: Vintage, 1987.

Nagurski-Bernstein, Irene. 'On a Soviet Edition of Doris Lessing's Stories'. *Doris Lessing Newsletter* 9.1 (Spring, 1985): 12.

'Presledovanie Pisatel'nitsi Doris Lessing'. *Komsomolskaya Pravda* 10 (5 October 1956): 3.

Sarukhanyan, A. P. 'Predislovie' (Preface). *No Witchcraft for Sale*. Moscow: Foreign Language Publishing House, 1956: iii–xv.

Smith, Lillian. *Killers of the Dream*. New York: W. W. Norton, 1949.

Vasil'eva, Larisa. 'Zhenshchina i Voina: "Uteshitel'nye" rassuzhdeniya Doris Lessing pod senyu yadernoi opasnosti'. *Literaturnaya Gazeta* 11 May 1983: 4.

Wilson, Robert Anton. 'The New Age Interview: Doris Lessing'. *New Age Journal* (January 1984): 30–3; 89–92.

Index

All references to Doris Lessing in this index have been abbreviated to DL.